GROW AND COOK

GROW AND COOK

MAKING THE MOST OF FOOD FROM
YOUR GARDEN

VIOLET STEVENSON

DAVID & CHARLES
NEWTON ABBOT LONDON
NORTH POMFRET (VT) VANCOUVER

ISBN 0 7153 6888 5

Library of Congress Catalog Card Number 75-2913

Set in 11 on 13pt Bembo and printed in
Great Britain by Latimer Trend & Company Ltd Plymouth
for David & Charles (Publishers) Limited
Brunel House Newton Abbot Devon

Published in the United States of America
by David & Charles Inc
North Pomfret Vermont 05053 USA

Published in Canada
by Douglas David & Charles Limited
1875 Welch Street North Vancouver BC

CONTENTS

FOREWORD

One night soon after we were married, Violet Stevenson and I were returning from a lecture tour in the north. We drove until late, planning to stay in a hotel which we knew and then complete our journey next day. But the hotel was full and we decided to drive through the night to get to our flat in Covent Garden in the early hours of the morning.

On the way Violet said in a small voice, 'There's nothing to eat at home, you know. I cleared the fridge before we left.' Our last meal had been a snack lunch and we were both famished.

When finally we arrived, before she even took off her coat, Violet filled a pan with water and put it on the stove. 'What are you doing?' I asked. 'Making some soup.' 'I thought you said the fridge was empty?' 'It is,' said Violet, showing it to me. I felt incredulity rather than hunger when I saw a handful of tapioca go in and a small tin of tomato extract and a spoonful of peanut butter and several more unlikely ingredients. All I now recall is that in about ten minutes I sat down to a huge bowl of the most delicious soup. Witchcraft, I thought. This is witchcraft.

Since then I have learned to be somewhat off-hand and casual about kitchen miracles, but visitors are inclined to be a little bemused. A typical comment, from a regular visitor over many years, 'Well, it's easy for you, Vi. You have such talent.'

Easy? I have known Violet get up at four in the morning in order to prepare an 'easy' meal. I have seen her struggle, head bent, across muddy fields in a gathering storm to collect the few delicate, wild lawyer's wig mushrooms before the rain spoiled them. I have seen her making bread at dawn so that her guests could have hot rolls for breakfast. I have seen her make up a recipe specially rich in vitamin B_{12} to tempt a sickly child's appetite and then make it up into dozens of toy-sized pancakes to attract his interest and amusement. I have heard her say, so many times, 'I don't know what it's called because it's never been made before.' And above all I have seen her in her vegetable garden, as functional as her kitchen, demanding and getting the best from her plants, always ready, even eager, to work beside them, to raise them in comfort and in health, to encourage them in their formative weeks and to bring them to the very second when they reach the peak of flavour and succulence and then—puff, into the pot!

There is no question about it, in our garden the vegetables belong to Violet. I am called in occasionally to carry out some heavy physical task or some unpleasant one such as murder, but otherwise I am allowed inside the huge fruit and vegetable cage only to admire. And this is, I think, as it should be. It is no good asking the man to grow the vegetables if he doesn't know how they should be cooked. It is no good expecting him to know exactly when the peas are sweetest, courgettes most succulent, radish most crisp and lettuce most nutty.

Let us have more cooks in the garden, for this way the vegetables will be better grown, with the emphasis on their flavour and their nutritional value rather than on their size. If the man grows the vegetables, then teach him to cook and he will grow them better.

It will be obvious from these few words that I should declare my interest. Declare it? I brag about it. The way to a man's heart, they say, is through his stomach. The enormity of my adoration is only too evident!

LESLIE JOHNS

INTRODUCTION

To me, growing vegetables is such a fundamental part of gardening that I cannot imagine owning a piece of land without endeavouring to produce some food on it. If all I had was a window-box and an indoor window-sill, I would have to grow herbs outside and mustard and cress indoors. And what was once merely a personal whim now seems to me to be a matter of expediency. Indeed, I would go so far as to say that anyone today who knows how to cultivate the soil and who has a plot of land no matter how tiny, has a duty to grow something to eat, no matter how small the contribution. It will be just that little bit less drawn from the store cupboard of a hungry world.

Whether it is because they share my views or whether it is more because they are sharing in a reaction against tasteless and characterless mass-produced foods, it is evident that there are more and more people who also want to produce some foods for themselves. The sale of vegetable seeds is higher than ever and is still growing.

Of course some of this interest is inspired by day-to-day economics. It saves you a lot of money if you grow some of your own food. Much of this saving arises from the fact that the food in your garden is there to start with, and you tend to plan menus from the basis of easily available foods. If you had to buy everything you would most likely consider the meats first, vegetables or fruit last of all, unless, that is, you were a vegetarian. When you grow your own you are likely to begin the other way round. It is surprising what a difference this makes. And, beginning from a 'Let's see what we have' basis is a much readier source of inspiration for the cook than is 'What shall we buy?' As a working wife, spending many hours a day at my own profession, I find it a tremendous help and a great time-saver always to have fresh vegetables in the garden with more, and fruit besides, in the freezer.

Nothing in the world tastes like the food you have harvested yourself. No shop tomato tastes like one you have just gathered. No lettuce is ever as crisp. No strawberries are so fragrant. If you are a good cook you will know also the joys of fresh leaf spinach, courgettes ad lib, cabbage so good that people actually ask for more, peas which seem to have no relationship with those that come from an ice-cold packet. Fresh vegetables need little cooking time to become tender; many are best raw. However, many do get spoiled in the cooking, simply, I think, because those who handle them haven't thought of them as something special.

Modern gardeners are beginning to realise that food crops do not have to be hefty. Small, neat, easily prepared and quickly grown roots, many of them now cylindrical and of even thickness, and tops such as cabbage and lettuce are more suitable for today's small families than the old bragged-about giants of the horticultural show bench. The hybridists have come to our aid here. More and more compact crops are being produced and with their neatness goes a quality known as 'longstanding'. In other words, summer lettuces upon forming tight hearts do not bolt or rush to flower as once they did, and cabbages will stay rock hard for weeks.

In many cases the desire to grow food is present but not the means. While there are many people, some for the first time in their lives, looking for an allotment or some extra little piece of land on which they can produce more food, there are many more who are studying the boundaries of their gardens, wondering how they can possibly find room for some vegetables or fruit without spoiling the look or character of the garden or undoing the hard work of many years.

Food crops need not spoil the appearance of a garden. Although it is more convenient to have a special kitchen garden set apart, there are also many ways and means of fitting fruit, vegetables and herbs into the decorative scheme of things. Visiting a friend's garden for the first time I was both surprised and enchanted to find that behind the waterfall cascading from a wall of rock, there existed a short but sufficient raspberry row and a salad garden. A pretty flower-filled garden I visited in another place had a ground cover of bright green lettuces among the roses in a border at the back of the house. My sister grew rows of spinach alongside a row of pinks bordering a garden path, and tripods of climbing beans among tall perennials.

A path border can easily be made productive as well as pretty. Parsley, alpine strawberries and lettuce will grow well in partial shade. The soil along a path is usually both moist and well drained, a good point in its favour. If you can raise the soil at the side of the path it will be warmer than if it were at the same level or below it. The only disadvantage about pathside planting occurs when espalier fruit trees are grown on the boundary of a fertile kitchen patch. Although this seems the obvious place to plant them, the trees often have access to too much nitrogenous food, given in the first place to the vegetable crops.

There are many neat, attractive and useful vegetables and herbs which can be mixed. Those which can be transplanted, such as lettuce, can be arranged in groups, just like flowering plants. For the small family there is Salad Bowl lettuce, which can be picked leaf by leaf, useful if you have to prepare daily sandwiches. If too many leaves are produced for daily use this way, they can always be cooked.

Crops which mature where they are sown can be made into attractive contrasting groups: for instance carrots, round beetroots, radishes, shallots, and herbs such as parsley, basil and chervil. Dual-purpose vegetables like greentop beetroots will provide leaves to cook as spinach and roots for salad. Swiss chard or seakale beet will provide such lush leaves that you can strip them and cook the green as spinach one day, the stems as seakale another. Hamburg parsley will give you leaves to use as a herb and roots to lift like parsnips. Red cabbage and sweet corn, purple-flowered peas and beans, will all look well with flowers. Tomatoes, aubergines and peppers can all be grown in pots, packs or other containers along a wall, cucumbers will climb a patio trellis, pumpkins and squash will cover a wall, bank or fence.

A kitchen patch can also be attractive in its own sturdy way, and a really useful quantity of food can be grown in quite a small area. I once designed a garden on view to the public. In one section of what was an average-sized suburban garden I had set aside a plot as a kitchen garden. It was covered entirely by netting as is my own personal kitchen garden. I love birds and animals but I like to keep them off my food crops. The kitchen plot in this public garden was no more than 16ft square. Yet here we grew a succession of vegetables the year through as well as some fruit for jams and preserves. Enough was produced to keep a small family well provided with everyday vegetables and fruit.

Apart from this strictly utilitarian patch (see plan opposite) certain

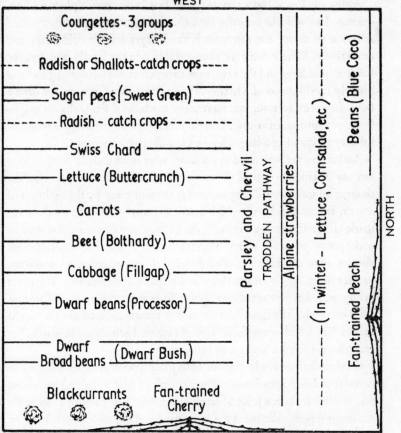

Courgettes - 3 groups

Radish or Shallots - catch crops

Sugar peas (Sweet Green)

Radish - catch crops

Swiss Chard

Lettuce (Buttercrunch)

Carrots

Beet (Bolthardy)

Cabbage (Fillgap)

Dwarf beans (Processor)

Dwarf Broad beans (Dwarf Bush)

Blackcurrants

Fan-trained Cherry

Parsley and Chervil

TRODDEN PATHWAY

Alpine strawberries

(In winter - Lettuce, Cornsalad, etc.)

Beans (Blue Coco)

NORTH

Fan-trained Peach

EAST

Summer plan for kitchen garden only 16ft square

useful plants were grown in other areas of the more decorative portions of the main garden. The most important was the Bramley apple tree which graced a corner of the lawn where its blossom could be seen from the house in spring, where it would give welcome shade in summer and where it would be easy to pick the fruit—and to watch over it—in autumn. Artichokes made handsome architectural plants in an odd corner where they received protection from an ornamental wall and where the soil had been made rich for them. Rhubarb flourished in a small site which occurred between two lots of paving. Here it could grow high, wide and handsome and was easy to reach from the house.

Although I deal with certain fruits briefly in their alphabetical sequences I would like to stress here that by planting a small yet varied selection of fruits one can stretch the budget both considerably and attractively. Where there are young children in the family, the desserts, the fruit puddings and the raw fruits themselves can become a good and homely food instead of a luxury. If you have a wall, a fence, or even a boundary wire or two, you have a site for trained fruit, always neighbours permitting, of course. Training fruit on a house wall is a wonderful way of winning a large area of valuable garden space.

And if you are interested in cooking, why limit fruit to dessert? You can use all kinds to extend the usefulness of other foods and to ring the changes ad infinitum. Many savouries are improved by the addition of certain fruits; pickles in which fruits are used prove this. Salads are made all the fresher by the inclusion of fruit and this is a good way to make more palatable a 'dry' vegetable such as shredded cabbage and also a way to cut down on salad dressing if you are either economising or slimming. Apple and cabbage is a popular combination. Try pears in any way that you serve raw apple. They are excellent peeled and on their own with salt ham. Use them in a prawn cocktail as you would melon. Try a tablespoonful or two of raw rhubarb slices cut wafer thin and mixed with a bland green mixture.

Cooked fruit can help eke out both joints and vegetables and add an unusual and delicious flavour. Put a couple of plums, halved and sliced side downwards on a joint of lamb when next you roast one. Sprinkle a little chopped garlic on at the same time and the merest sprinkling of brown sugar. When you roast parsnips with pork, bake a few apples too; all three go well together. As a savoury with meat, core unpeeled apples and stuff them with chopped shallot and the appropriate herb—rosemary for lamb, for instance—and bake whole. Gooseberries make a good sauce for fish. Poached gently in a little honey and kept whole, these too can be used in a salad. They are good with potato salad and tarragon. Put a few mixed berries into an autumn salad—good with red cabbage, and pretty too. Mix cherries with cauliflower.

If you find that you can grow only very few vegetables, then do make sure that you get every ounce of value from them. The water in which they are cooked, for a start, is the basis of an excellent soup. This contains all the minerals drawn from the food during cooking and so is rich in food value. It is also money and labour saving. Often all you have to do, if the quantity is sufficient, is to thicken it in the way you like best, garnish it prettily with fresh chopped herbs or perhaps finely chopped radish and baby carrots, and serve. I like to throw in a whole garlic clove and a bay leaf, both removed later, to flavour the stock as it comes again to the boil.

Often, much more of the vegetable plant can be eaten than the average shopper realises. Take cauliflowers for instance; what happens to all those fine leaves which grow around the curd? The greengrocer cuts them off and throws them away. But they can be used as greens. Those nearest the curd are the most tender, but even the tough outer ones can be shredded and boiled and the liquor used to make an excellent cauliflower cream soup. The same applies to Brussels sprouts. When the sprouts are gathered, the leaves in whose axils the sprouts grow can be used if greens are scarce. The tops, left till last, make fine spring greens.

Onion, shallot, garlic and leek tops can all be used either to flavour sauces, stocks and soups, or actually included in some. Peascods or pods make excellent soup and purée. The tough outer leaves of lettuce can be cooked either alone, with an onion or two (green tops included) or with spinach. Bolting lettuces can be braised. The thick stem can be peeled and sliced and used like cucumber.

Spinach and beet leaves, radish tops (my father loved to eat them as a salad, well laced with dressing), thinnings from rows of brassicas, chicory, lettuce and tips of pinched-out broad bean plants can all be used for nutritious and—if you wish—slimming soups.

But don't take it for granted that if a plant's root, and in some cases its stem, is wholesome its leaves will be edible also. This is not the case. Never eat, for example, the leaves of rhubarb, parsnips, potatoes, tomatoes or carrots. Don't experiment without asking advice if you are not sure.

Seeds are remarkably cheap. Many packets contain far too much seed for the average small garden, or at least there is far too much if all the seeds germinate and all the seedlings survive the ravages of slugs and other pests. Some vegetables should be sown where they are to mature. Others can be transplanted. It is sometimes worth while to share these with a neighbouring gardener.

It is important to sow thinly, simply because it saves you so much time later and because it gives the uncrowded seedlings a good start in life. The most important factor in raising succulent vegetables is that they should grow quickly. Many vegetable seeds are now individually pelleted with a thick coating of plant foods, moisture attractors and ingredients which protect the young seedling from pests and diseases and so give it a good start in life. As the seeds germinate the coating disintegrates. Naturally these pellets are much larger than the seeds they contain, which means that they can be handled and sown individually, thus saving the chore and waste of thinning out later. Only some kinds and varieties are yet available and these include beet, carrot, lettuce, onion, parsnip and leek.

Obviously, if you want to get the greatest value from your little bit of land you should keep it filled. This implies that the soil must be in good heart, well fed and constantly enriched. One of the best ways of doing this and of cutting out labour in the form of weeding and watering is to mulch well between the rows of vegetables. As I have a large area of lawn I use deep mulches of lawn mowings. I also use well-rotted animal manure and a little, though never very much, of a good all-round chemical fertiliser. There is no need to spend much money this way if you are working to a strict budget. Simply bear in mind that the garden is like a bank account, you cannot keep drawing from it without putting something in. All the vegetable refuse you fail to eat or which cannot be eaten should be composted along with all other vegetable trimmings from other parts of the garden, and then, when it is in good condition, returned to the soil, which it will help to improve both in richness and in all-important texture.

Another item which greatly increases the potential productivity of a garden is a deep freeze. If you install one of these you will be able to produce much more in the same area of soil as you can clear a crop so much more quickly. Instead of waiting until you have eaten your way through, say, a row of cauliflowers, you can set aside an hour or two in the kitchen and deal with the entire row at one time, and while the plants are at the height of perfection. This means that on the next day the soil can be prepared and a new crop either sown or planted, thus growing two crops in the space normally occupied by one.

And finally, after food, drink. It seems to me that most of my neighbours make home-made wines of some kind or another, and although personally I prefer the wines of that little area around Reims in northern France more than any other drink in the world, in our family also we manufacture certain wines from the garden and the hedgerow. There is no doubt, after many years, that I find these wines most useful is in cooking.

In case the reader is not experienced in wine making I have included some basic directions as well as some recipes, but I would like to add that a visit to a chemist or a shop which specialises in items for this hobby is advisable as well as interesting. Equipment of all kinds, yeasts and recipes abound and are inexpensive. There are also wine circles and societies where the experienced are always willing to help the initiates.

Note: In all recipes which follow a cup is equal to half a pint.

ANGELICA

Growing

Here's a handsome plant, up to 5ft tall with wide leaves and greenish-white flowers. It's ideal for the gardener who is planning to make a plot both beautiful and productive. It does best on an alkaline soil, but this needs to be rich and loamy. The plant grows best in light shade. You can buy potted plants or raise your own from packeted seed. Sow this in March in the place where it is to grow. Thin out the plants when they are about 3in high. These can be transplanted.

Always leave one flower to go to seed. Fresh seed seems to germinate best. Sow this as soon as it is ripe. Your own seedlings and those you find growing around the parent plant will transplant better than larger plants you buy. You will also have some to give away.

Angelica is a biennial. It is possible to coax it to act as a perennial if it is prevented from flowering, but this is a pity in some ways because the great globular umbels are so distinctive and handsome.

Cooking

All parts of the plant are fragrant and the herb is sweet to the taste, so much so that it is used in confectionary. Stems are candied and used to decorate cakes and other sweetmeats. These very large stems are taken from plants which have been prevented from flowering, and which are usually about three years old. The entire stem is used, cut into conveniently sized portions.

The peeled stems at any age are good to eat, nibbled raw like celery or sliced and mixed in salads. Roots also are edible, not unlike Hamburg parsley. The seeds can be used for flavouring and for pot-pourri.

Angelica goes very pleasantly with rhubarb, giving it a delicious flavour; 3 parts of rhubarb to 1 of angelica will do. Try it in a pie.

Angelica and Rhubarb Jam

Allow 3 parts rhubarb to 1 part tender angelica stems. Cut each into sections of about 1in length. Weigh or measure an equal quantity of sugar. Use a heavy pan and very little water. Simmer the angelica until it is tender. Add the rhubarb. Stir until the sugar melts. Simmer slowly. Test after 15min or so if you do not use a thermometer. Rhubarb sometimes takes a long time to gel. Hasten this process by using pectin.

Candied Angelica

This takes time and patience but many people think it well worth while. It is useful to have at hand a good stock of such attractive and unusual confectionary. You might have enough to give as presents.

The best time to candy angelica is in April or early May while the stalks are tender. Cut the thick stem into convenient lengths. The usual length is 3–4in, but there is no set rule, and if longer, they may be difficult to store.

Wash the stems. Leave them to soak in cold water for 1hr. Boil a pan of water. Using a vegetable blancher or a chip basket lower the stem pieces into this and let them remain there as the water simmers until they are tender. They should just give when lightly pressed. Cool them in cold water, drain and peel them carefully. As you remove the peel you will find the stem fibres, stringy pieces, and you must be sure to remove these. Lay the stems on a dish.

Make a syrup of sugar, 1 cup of sugar to 1 cup of water. Increase these quantities if this amount does not cover the stems. Let them remain together for 24hr. Drain off the syrup and cook it until it reaches 225° F, 105° C. Pour it back over the stems. Repeat this operation over 3 consecutive days. Finally, bring the syrup up to 245° F, 125° C. When it reaches this temperature place the angelica in it and boil it until it becomes clear. The old recipe I originally consulted said that one should bring it to the boil several times. I think that this is better than prolonging the boiling at one time. When the angelica looks candied, let it cool in its syrup. Take it out, drain it on a sieve. When dry, sprinkle each piece with fine sugar, lay them on a sieve and let them dry slowly in a barely warm oven. Do not overdo this or the angelica may become tough and rubbery. Store between pieces of greaseproof paper in tins or airtight plastic food boxes.

Don't waste the syrup. Bottle it and use it in small quantities for sweetening and flavouring fruit salads or other dishes.

Once you have candied the angelica you will find many uses for it. Not so obvious, perhaps, is its inclusion in fresh fruit salads. Cut some very thinly and mix with the fruit.

I use angelica for decorating Christmas cakes, instead of bought decorations. It is possible to slice through thick pieces of candied stem, making several thin sections from one piece. Use a sharp pointed knife and have a cup of hot water at hand. Dip the knife in the water before cutting a new slice. From these sections I cut out ivy, holly and mistletoe leaves. I use a tiny ivy leaf, a soft and pliable holly leaf and a single mistletoe leaf as patterns. These are laid on thin board. I pencil around the leaf outlines and cut out the shapes. It is then quite easy to cut them out from the angelica. Use a pointed knife and follow the pattern.

When these leaf shapes are laid on white royal icing they look both wholesome and attractive. You can make a garland of ivy all around the cake and around part of the edge and cluster the holly and mistletoe inside. To give really good contrast, make berries from glacé cherries, red ones for holly, yellow for mistletoe and green for ivy. Cut each cherry into pieces of suitable size.

APPLES

Growing

Try to find room at least for a cooking apple if not for a dessert variety. If you are looking for a handsome tree for the lawn you can't do better than plant an apple, a Bramley Seedling, for example. This will give lovely scented blossom in the spring, shade in summer, fruit for autumn and winter and a pleasant outline to admire in winter.

If you have space alongside a garden path or even across a plot where their shade will be no detriment, you can grow a row of cordon apples, single stemmed plants. These need careful and regular pruning to keep them under control. Arched cordons reaching over garden paths, even a path which runs along a house, are beautifully decorative and great space savers. There are also 'bushes', pyramids and half-standards for those who do not want a full-sized tree.

Cooking

Don't be limited to sweet dishes, for apples can be savoury too. Try them baked whole with meats—sugar baked ham, for instance. Apples are especially good with duck and goose and are excellent in salads. If you think your apples are a little too sharp when eaten raw, mix some raisins, sultanas or currants with them. Try apple with chopped mint and a little sugar. Apples make good fritters, but instead of limiting these to puddings, try them with pork chops or fried chicken. Fry apples in rings with bacon for breakfast and so save on grapefruit. Windfalls can be used in pickles, chutneys, cider, wine, jams, jellies, or simply puréed and frozen or bottled.

For an easily prepared meal I sometimes make layers of gammon, onion slices and apple, in that order, in a buttered oven dish. A light sprinkling of brown sugar is made over each triple decker layer and I also add a sage leaf. This is then covered and baked in a slow oven for an hour or so. If you have to delay the meal, simply lower the temperature. Serve with jacket potatoes.

Much the same mixture can be used as a pie, in which case you can use smaller pieces of lean bacon.

Apples and tomatoes have much in common in the way that they can be cooked and used. Try them together in

Potted Pork Chops and Kidneys (serves 6)

6 small pork chops
2 pigs' kidneys finely sliced
½lb apples quartered and finely sliced
4 or 5 juniper berries crushed
2 shallots finely sliced
1 large clove garlic finely chopped

½lb tomatoes or equivalent in purée
2tsp freshly chopped sage
mustard
1lb onions sliced
1½lb potatoes sliced
cupful (½pt) of good stock
½ cup red wine (optional)
seasoning

Mix juniper, apples, shallots, garlic, tomatoes, sage, seasoning together. Smear mustard on each side of chops—a fine tenderiser as well as a flavouring. In a deep casserole make a layer of onions and potatoes and on this place three chops. Lay the slices of one kidney on these and sprinkle on half the apple and tomato mixture. Repeat the process with the other half of the ingredients. Add stock and wine. Cover. Cook in a slow oven for 3hr. This dish will not suffer if it has to stay in the oven a little longer. This is a good dinner party dish because you can make it well in advance. Serve with a crisp salad.

Apple and Mint Lamb Loaf (serves 6)

Breast of lamb
to flavour:

1 small onion
shallot
clove garlic
bouquet garni and any pot herbs

you may have such as celery stalk, leek, carrot, parsnip, lovage
add salt

For the jelly:

1oz powdered gelatine
2tbsp lemon juice (vinegar can be used but I don't like it so much)
1 heaped tbsp finely chopped

mint (don't do this until the last moment so that you retain the full flavour)
1 heaped tbsp finely diced apple
salt and pepper

Cut the lamb into two to three pieces so that it fits well into a saucepan. Add the salt, vegetables and herbs and cover with water. Bring all slowly to the boil and then let this simmer very slowly for some hours until the lamb is tender, but not overdone or it will be 'ragged'. The more slowly it is cooked the better. Leave overnight to cool.

Remove the meat, take off the fat from stock and set this aside. While you are cutting the meat reheat the stock. Add it to the bones and the pieces of skin taken from the meat. You will need 1pt of stock for the loaf, so add more water at this point if necessary. Cut the meat tidily. Set aside any fatty pieces; these can be rendered down later. Unlike pork, lamb fat in a jelly is not appetising.

When you are ready, put the gelatine in a basin and mix it with 2tbsp cold water. Pour the stock over this through a strainer. Mix well. Let it cool and then add the lemon, mint, apple, salt and pepper. Mix these ingredients well, taste and adjust the seasoning if necessary. Chill the mixture, but do not allow it to set too much. Add the lamb. Have ready a mould. Pour in the mixture and chill it until it is well set. Turn it out on a dish well garnished with more mint. Delicious with home-made brown bread.

Open Apple Cake

4oz fat	4 medium sized cooking apples,
10oz self-raising flour	or enough to cover pastry
4oz fine sugar	quartered and neatly sliced
good pinch salt	3tbsp milk
1 egg	1tsp cinnamon

Rub the fat into the flour, add salt and 2oz sugar. Beat egg up in milk and mix into the dough. Flour the hands and a Swiss-roll tin. Roll the pastry to the approximate size of the tin and press it into it, taking the pastry up the sides so as to make a little pastry tray.

Cut the apples into slices, orange-segment shaped, and arrange these across the dough in attractive rows. Mix remaining 2oz sugar with the cinnamon and sprinkle this over the apples. Bake at 425° F, 220° C for 25–30min. Leave it in tin to cool.

Make this into a party dish by topping it with white of egg beaten up with sugar. In this case use the yolk for the pastry and the white for the topping. You may need to add a little more milk.

Apple Ginger

3lb apples
5 or 6 cloves
2 lemons
1tsp ground ginger

1pt water
12oz sugar for each 1lb apple pulp
12oz preserved ginger (in syrup)

Peel, core and slice the apples fairly thickly, quarters might do if you are using small apples. Save the peel and cores so long as these are not blemished and put them with the cloves in a muslin or nylon bag. Peel the lemons finely with a potato peeler. Put the peel and juice with the ground ginger, apples, water and bag and its contents into a preserving pan.

Bring slowly to the boil and cook until the apples are quite soft. Squash the bag down from time to time to soften its contents. Remove the bag, stroke it with a wooden spoon so that you get all the juice from it. Weigh the apple pulp. Add the sugar and the ginger cut into small pieces. Boil all together until the preserve sets, which should be about 20–30min.

Apple Wine

This is a delightful wine to serve slightly chilled with a meal. No need to use best apples. Save skin and cores from pie and stewed apples; these will keep some days in refrigerator or freezer. Use any apples that have been marked or bruised. Mix as many kinds as you can, including crab apples from the flowering crabs if you have them. A few quince from your japonica give a delicious flavour and aroma.

6lb chopped apple
rind and juice of 1 lemon
3lb white sugar

yeast
8oz seedless raisins minced or chopped, added later

Boil apples and lemon rind in 1gal water until soft, about 15min. Strain into a bucket over the sugar. When lukewarm add the lemon juice and the prepared yeast. Cover well and leave to ferment for 24hr.

Pour all into a fermenting jar, leave for 4 weeks and then rack off into a clean jar. Add the raisins. Insert an airlock and leave until you are sure that fermentation has ceased. Cork and leave for 6 months, then rack into bottles.

ARTICHOKES

Growing

Make a feature of these handsome plants. Grow them in an open, sunny place in groups of three, 2ft apart. It is best to buy plants, as seeds are often variable. Plant in April in really rich, deep soil, well-manured. Water well during their first season. Protect plants from November to early March by heaping peat, chopped bracken or similar dry litter over them. Mulch in March with well-rotted manure or home-made compost, or if you live near the coast use seaweed. During summer give established plants liquid manure. Never let them get dry at the roots.

If you have a large garden with room for rows of artichokes, you can grow them on a three-year rotation, French style. In March or April examine the plants in your one row and reduce the number of shoots or suckers so that you leave only three. These should produce really large heads. You have to scrape the soil away from around the plant to see these. Cut the shoot with a portion of root. Use these to make another, second row. Next year repeat the process and so on. After the 3-year-old plants have cropped, throw them away. (This excellent and money-saving method is the suggestion of my friend Roy Hay, to whom I am indebted.)

Cooking globe artichokes

The great buds of this plant are the parts eaten. The scales or bracts, called 'leaves' in cookery, are pulled off one by one, their ends dipped in sauce or butter and the succulent bases sucked. The leaves become less fleshy as the petals or 'choke' is reached, but under these is the delicious heart which can be eaten with knife and fork. When the flowers are young and the choke still tender they can be simply eaten raw with salt.

More usually they are cooked and served with melted butter or vinaigrette, either hot or cold. After boiling them whole you can also scoop out the tough choke carefully leaving the heart below and stuff the centre with a variety of good things.

Whole Artichokes Boiled

Cut the stalks to the base. Pull off the two or three really tough outer leaves. If the buds are very long, trim the leaf tips with scissors. Place, base downwards, in boiling salted water and boil for 30–45min. Test by pressing the base, which should give, or alternatively by pulling at a leaf. When cooked this should come away easily. Don't overcook or you will lessen the flavour.

Serve hot with the sauce of your choice.

Braised Artichokes with Bacon

4 artichokes	8 rashers streaky bacon

For fillings:

1oz butter	2oz finely chopped ham or
1 medium onion	bacon
2 shallots, both finely chopped	1tbsp chopped parsley
4oz mushrooms, finely chopped	knob of butter
salt, pepper, nutmeg	wine glass white wine

Melt 1oz butter, lightly brown the onion and shallots, add mushrooms, salt and pepper to taste and a generous sprinkling of nutmeg. Cook briskly, stirring well so that all liquid evaporates as the mixture cooks. Remove from heat and add the ham or bacon and parsley. Meanwhile, boil the artichokes. Remove chokes. Tie the rashers around them, two to each. Divide the filling between the four. Fill the centres. Melt enough butter in a heavy pan to cover the bottom, pour in the wine and stand the artichokes in the pan. Bake for 1hr at 350° F, 180° C.

Carefully lift the artichokes on to a dish, cover with foil and keep warm while making a sauce with the liquor in the pan. First skim off any surplus fat, add some good stock and let this evaporate until it is well flavoured with the other juices in the pan. Alternatively, begin with 1tbsp sherry and bring to the boil. Serve in a separate sauce boat.

Growing Jerusalem artichokes

Although these plants are also members of the daisy tribe, they do not resemble the globe artichoke. They are *Helianthus tuberosus*, tall, 5ft sunflowers, often to be seen in a mass in the corner of some old garden. They do not demand a special site, nor a row across a plot, and can be tucked away in any odd spot of rich soil. Jerusalem artichokes make good summer screens between one area of garden and another.

As can be guessed from the name, it is the tuberous roots and not the flowers which are eaten. It is sometimes difficult to find the 'seed' tubers on sale, but those you buy from the vegetable shops will do. Try to get a French variety, Fusean, whose tubers are more regular in shape. Dig the ground well in advance and manure it generously. Plant the tubers early, in February if possible, or any time in winter so long as the soil is workable, 18in apart in rows 3ft apart.

Let the plants flower and cut them down in late autumn, leaving a few inches of stem so that you can see where the tubers are. These are best left in the soil and dug as required. If they are out of the ground for long they tend to become shrivelled and dry. If you think that this may offer problems, lift some from time to time and store them in boxes of dry peat in a shed.

Set aside some tubers for seed and replant anew at any time during winter.

Cooking Jerusalem artichokes

Their flavour is considered to be best after the shortest day.

The tubers can be exasperating to prepare if they are very irregular. I find a coarse nail-brush is as good as anything in getting them really clean. Scrub them well and then cook in boiling water for about 5min, just long enough to make it easy to peel them after cooling under running water. After this cook them in the way the recipe directs.

Jerusalem artichokes are simply and deliciously cooked in butter with very little water. They are also especially good when served in a bechamel-type sauce with fish or meat. The liquid in which they are cooked is so well flavoured that this should always be used for the sauce. You can make it whiter and richer by adding cream.

Artichoke Tarts

Cook and add to a fairly thick sauce then pour into a pre-cooked, ready-warm pastry pie case, or perhaps small individual cases. Lightly cover the top with grated Parmesan cheese and a little nutmeg and brown under a grill.

Artichoke Soufflé (serves 4)

1 cup (½pt) purée (drain and then blend or sieve the artichokes)	¼pt double cream 2 eggs seasoning

Put the purée in a saucepan with the cream and blend well together. Do not let the liquid become too hot. Season with black pepper and salt. It is always advisable to taste, especially if you have used salted butter. On the other hand remember that soufflés, because of the amount of egg white in them, usually need a more highly flavoured seasoning than many other dishes.

Remove the pan from the fire and let it cool a little. Make sure that the oven is ready. Separate 2 eggs and blend in the yolks with the purée. Mix well. Beat the whites until firm and fold into the mixture.

I find that much time and washing-up is saved if a fairly large saucepan is used for the purées or sauces from which soufflés are to be made and then this will serve as the only mixing utensil. The whites are sometimes difficult to fold in, but you should never beat them. Using a large spoon cut the mixture criss-cross with it and fold. Work quickly, but don't panic. I once found that I had put soufflés in the oven without their yolks, so I quickly removed them, tipped them out, remixed and replaced them in the oven. The gamble succeeded. Use a spatula to take every scrap of mixture from the sides of the pan.

I have stopped making soufflés in large dishes and then doling them out when cooked as the soufflé always seems to suffer. I much prefer to make individual dishes. However, whether large or small, fill the dish just three-quarters full. Cook in a moderate oven around 375° F, 190° C. Large soufflés need 20–25min, small ones 8–10min. These are best stood on a baking sheet or in a Swiss-roll tin for easy handling. Butter the dishes first.

Judging when, or if, a soufflé is done is not always easy, but the

26

advantage of small soufflés is that they will go on cooking while the dishes are being served. Better not quite ready than overdone.

Artichoke Salad

Cook and slice. While the vegetable is still warm pour over it a little white wine. Later serve with vinaigrette or mayonnaise.

ASPARAGUS

Growing

One mistake I made when planning my own kitchen garden was to let some years pass before making an asparagus bed. Since you have to wait three years after planting mature roots before the grass should be cut, my advice is that if you want to ensure full value from your plot, plan for this crop from the beginning. I was put off by the traditional method of growing asparagus, in 4ft wide beds with 2ft paths or alleys between them as I did not have such space to spare. If you have, then go ahead and follow the rules, but what I have done is to plant one long row in a narrow raised bed which runs alongside the path that goes through the vegetable garden. This same border is edged with strawberry plants. I never have a great crop of spears, but I have enough to make their growing worth while, and the plants produce more each year.

Although asparagus can be raised from seed, after which the seedlings are planted in their permanent positions when they are in their second or third year, I think that it is better in the long run to buy 3-year-old plants from a specialist grower. Male plants produce a larger crop of shoots, and these are more surely selected by an expert than by a novice. Incidentally, plants which produce berries are the female plants, and as these produce slender, weaker spears, they are best rooted out and replaced by males. When plants are raised from seed they can be culled and the females discarded.

Plant the asparagus 18in apart. A double row can have the plants 18in apart each way. If you grow two double rows allow 4ft between them. Plant in late March or April. Don't be in too great a hurry, the warmer the soil the quicker the plants will grow. Get the roots into the soil and covered as quickly as possible. Try not to expose them to the drying air.

Naturally the soil should already be well prepared. If you are an energetic gardener you can take out a trench the length of the row, making it 9in deep and 9in wide. Insert a cane to show where each plant should go. Line the base of the trench with some nicely rotted compost if you have it for the depth of at least 1in, and around each cane make a little heap some 4in high. If you have no good compost, mix a little good soil for this purpose, adding a little peat and sand, some fertiliser and even some burnt earth if the soil is heavy.

You will find that the asparagus crowns have soft, string-like roots. Sit the plants on the little heaps you have made and spread these roots out, handling them carefully so that they cap and even cover the mounds. I suggest that you leave the cane in place at first. You can remove them once the spears grow. Cover the roots of each plant immediately. Sprinkle a little fertiliser in the trench ready to nourish the growing plants. Have a mixture of 2 parts superphosphate and 1 part sulphate of potash ready to use. Apply this at a rate of 1oz per 1yd length of row. Fill in the trench. The crowns of the plants should be well covered with about 4–5in of soil.

If taking out a whole trench is too much work for you, follow much the same method but simply remove the soil at each station, attending to one plant only at a time. Firm the soil by treading it lightly.

From now on keep the bed free from weeds. The deep digging in preparation probably will have brought many weed seeds to the surface, so eradicate these as soon as they germinate. Do not cut out any spears the first year. Cut down the 'grass' as soon as the foliage turns yellow in the autumn. Then give the bed a good mulch, 2–3in of well-rotted farmyard manure or a good home-made garden compost.

The next spring, clean the bed and sprinkle it with agricultural or even common salt at a rate of 1oz per sq yd. Continue this routine annually. Begin cutting the shoots in the third year. They should be about 3in above soil level. Take a sharp knife, or a specially designed asparagus knife if you can buy one, and push it obliquely into the soil at the side of the shoot so that you cut it some 4in below the soil surface. Cut all shoots as they are ready, and see that all those which grow in the period from their first appearance until about midsummer day are cut. After this any that appear can be left to mature.

When cutting is finished, fertilise the soil by mixing together 5 parts superphosphate, 2 parts sulphate of potash, 1 part sulphate of ammonia and apply at the rate of 9oz per sq yd. Alternatively, use a good general fertiliser.

Cooking

When your first shy spears appear above the ground you may not have enough to make a dish but these will keep well in the refrigerator for a few days while more grow. I store mine in a lidded plastic box.

To boil, peel or scrape the pale end of the stalks, then wash well making sure that there is no grit in the tips. Traditionally they are then cut into equal lengths and tied into small bundles before being lowered into plenty of boiling salted water. I prefer not to tie mine but put them into the pan, tips all one way, and then when done I lift them out with a fish slice.

If the asparagus is to be served cold the drained spears are usually either dipped into cold water or held under running water to cool them, but I prefer to leave them in the water to cool in their own juice as it were, which adds flavour. In this case I cook them for 15min and then turn off the heat. Asparagus should never be overcooked—18–20min is enough for freshly gathered spears.

Green Asparagus Sauce

If you are fussy about trimming the shoots so that they are all of the same length and look professionally uniform, you are sure to be left with some odds and ends that are much too good to waste. Try making a green asparagus sauce with them. You can use the not-so-good spears in this also.

This sauce is delicious with cold chicken, salmon, shrimps, prawns, other fish and indeed anything which is not so highly flavoured itself that it kills the taste of the asparagus. It can be served hot or cold.

First cook the pieces in as little water as possible. Make a bechamel sauce from butter, flour, asparagus water and chicken stock or, if you are serving fish, with a stock made from the fish trimmings. Chop the asparagus into fairly uniform pieces and add to the sauce together with a dash of paprika and nutmeg. If the sauce is to be served cold, so that it does not form a skin, cover and cool.

You can use this sauce to cover and garnish a whole, cold, boiled chicken. Let the sauce cool until it is just warm and will flow a little, then spoon it over the chicken so that it is entirely coated. Stand it in the refrigerator to set well before serving.

When trimming the spears do not waste those tough pale ends, even if they are short. They hold a lot of flavour. Peel them and cut the inner portion into segments. Cook them in a little boiling water and, when done, incorporate them in salads and sauces.

Asparagus à la Flamande

Some Dutch friends introduced us to this dish of asparagus and hard-boiled eggs, both served hot with the eggs on a separate dish. Each person takes an egg and mashes it well with a fork, blending in a little melted butter, then eats the tips with it.

On the premise that these three foods—hard-boiled eggs, butter and asparagus—go well together, I made the following light dish from hard-boiled eggs and odds and ends of asparagus. Shell and halve the eggs lengthwise. Lay then in a shallow oven dish. Make a bechamel sauce using the water in which the asparagus was boiled and extra milk or cream to bring it to the required quantity. When it thickens add the diced or sliced asparagus. Pour this over the eggs. Sprinkle the top lightly with a little Parmesan cheese and dot the surface with butter. Brown under the grill.

Jellied Asparagus

This is a good way of using just a few tips. Have ready some good consommé made from chicken bones. Make sure that it has been cooked sufficiently so that it will gel when cold, and if not add a little gelatine. Season. Arrange the asparagus in little ramekins and pour the liquid over.

If you have a freezer
To keep asparagus in a deep freeze, blanch small spears for 2min and larger ones for 3min. Asparagus becomes softer after freezing and is best eaten with a fork, not picked up in the fingers.

AUBERGINES

Growing

In warm Mediterranean lands rows and rows of aubergines or egg-plants are grown almost casually, in little plots of land, even in strips between blocks of vines. They will grow out of doors in Britain too, but generally you will be more successful if you grow them in pots against a warm, sunny, sheltered wall or fence. Of course so much depends upon your locality. If you can grow tomatoes well, then go ahead with your aubergines. Hybridists have been busy and have produced early-maturing varieties such as 'Short Tom'. Cloches can be used to protect the plants in the early days of summer. Use them also to ward off cool winds.

Aubergines like plenty of light and are a good crop for the cool greenhouse or the conservatory. The seed needs to be sown in warmth, 55°–65° F, 13°–19° C. Less work is involved if it is sown singly into small pots, 2½in diameter is a good size. Failing this, prick out the seedlings as soon as you can handle them and syringe them daily with clean, tepid water. Do not let the roots become dry.

Once the pots are filled with roots, repot the plants in larger containers, using a good potting compost—when established and growing away they can be stood in a cool house or, in June, outdoors. Water the plants generously. When they are about 6in high they should be 'stopped', that is, their growing tips should be pinched out so that they will produce many shoots down the stem. You can feed aubergines with any good specialist tomato fertiliser such as Tomorite.

It is best to restrict the fruits so that each plant carries no more than half a dozen or so.

Cooking

Aubergines vary in shape according to the variety, being long or round. The majority are a deep purple, but others are whitish and even striped. There appears to be no difference in their flavour.

Stuffed Aubergines

These are excellent vegetables for all 'farcies' recipes. Basically the procedure is the same. Cut the aubergine in half lengthwise, fry in sizzling olive oil cut-side downwards until the flesh is tender but the skin is still firm. Remove it from the oil and carefully scoop out the pulp with a spoon leaving the skin intact.

Mash the flesh and blend with the filling which should always be well seasoned and, in my view, well flavoured with garlic. Indeed, I fry a little garlic in the pan with the halves. You can use any minced or finely chopped cooked meats, sausage meats, left-over turkey, rice, mushrooms, pepper, tomato and onion mixtures, shrimps or other fish, chopped hard-boiled eggs, foods in a thick bechamel, or whatever you wish. Replace the filling inside the skins. Sprinkle the tops with fine breadcrumbs, dotted with butter and bake or grill. Alternatively, place grated Parmesan cheese or a slice of some more gooey cheese, Emmental for instance, on the top and bake or grill the whole dish.

If you prefer it, you can blanch the aubergines in boiling salted water for 10min instead of frying them before scooping out the flesh and stuffing them.

Aubergine Soufflés

You can use the above farcies method to make aubergine soufflés which makes a good starter to a dinner party.

Have the skins ready in a heatproof dish. Chop the pulp finely, or blend it or rub it through a sieve. Stir it into equal quantities of a thick bechamel sauce. To every ¼pt pulp allow 2 eggs. Add the egg yolks. Blend these in while the mixture is warm but not hot. Season well. Whisk the egg whites until they stand firm. Fold them into the mixture. Fill the skins. Sprinkle each with a topping of finely grated Parmesan cheese (optional but it does make a lovely, brown, crisp topping) and a generous sprinkling of nutmeg. Bake in a moderate oven for 8–10min. Serve at once.

Grilled Aubergine Slices

Use these as individual bases for other cooked foods—for instance, top them with any of the farcies mixtures, or simply serve them as a vegetable with ham, lamb, chicken, rice or bacon.

Cut slices nearly 1in thick. Lay them in a shallow heatproof dish. Brush each surface with a little olive oil and sprinkle lightly with salt. Place the dish under the grill and let the slices cook slowly for 15min. Turn each slice and repeat the process. You can, if you wish, grill them quickly until brown and then bake them for the remainder of the time.

Aubergine Salad

A Spanish salad can be made from baked aubergines and peppers. Try to use both red and green peppers to give the dish good colour. There are no precise quantities. Put all in an oven dish with a little olive oil. Cover the dish and bake slowly until the contents are tender, roughly 30min in a moderate oven. Cool and skin. Cut into rough slices. Garnish with chopped parsley and dress with a lemon juice and oil dressing.

B

BASIL

Growing (see Herbs)

If you like Italian cooking you cannot really get by without this spicy, pungent herb. There are two species grown, both of them half-hardy annuals. Sweet basil, the more popular of the two is *Ocimum basilicum* and is 12in tall. It has given rise to a handsome, dark-leaved, almost black variety known as Dark Opal. This is splendid enough for parks gardeners to use it in some of their spectacular bedding schemes. Its leaves are usefully pungent, although perhaps not so attractive on certain dishes as the green. I would always have both, the species and the variety.

The other species is the little Bush Basil (*O. minimum*) which grows to about 6in high.

Sow seeds of both species indoors during March or April. Prick out the seedlings into small individual pots and then plant them out when they are a good size in late May or early June after they have been properly hardened.

You can keep a few back to grow on a window-sill or in a greenhouse if you have one. These plants will mature faster and you will soon be able to use them. At first rob each one only a little. Later, when they are larger, you can cut them a little harder. When finally they no longer look their best, you can if you wish take the plants outdoors, plunge them up to their pot rims in the soil and let them remain to recuperate. Water and feed them from time to time, lift them at the end of summer and bring them indoors again.

Also for autumn and winter supplies you can lift good plants from the borders at the end of summer in the same way that you would lift a pelargonium or geranium. Water them in well after potting. Do not choose too large a pot, squeeze the roots into one which just fits.

Leave the plants standing in a sheltered place for a few days to settle down. Remove faded leaves and pinch off any flowers and then bring them into the greenhouse or the home.

The soil for basil needs to be ordinary, neither specially peaty nor limy, but it should be rich and the plant located in a sunny position. Beware of slugs when you put out the young plants. In my experience they make a beeline (if this is zoologically possible) for the seedlings.

Cooking (see also Herbs)
Extra pungent, smelling slightly of clove but with a distinctive aroma all its own, basil is, or can be, used in all savoury dishes which include tomato. It is *the* herb for pizzas. Basil is also a bean herb and can be served chopped on all beans, fresh or dried. It enlivens all the members of the marrow family, whether these be plain marrow or squash, courgettes or zuccini.

Courgettes with Basil (serves 4)

1lb courgettes, washed and sliced into 1in sections	1tbsp chopped green or red pepper
1 small onion sliced	1tsp salt
1 small shallot	good helping of freshly ground black pepper
1 garlic clove chopped	1 bay leaf
2tbsp olive oil	1tsp chopped basil
2 tomatoes, peeled, pipped and chopped	

Heat oil in heavy pan. Add onion, shallot and garlic, cover and let these 'melt'. Oil should not be allowed to get too hot. Add tomatoes and peppers. Cover and cook for about 5min. Add courgettes and seasoning and bay leaf. Cover and cook for a further 20min. Add basil, cook for another 5min.

Polenta with Basil (serves 6)

$\frac{3}{4}$ cup of polenta (maize meal)

2 cups (1pt) of milk

bay leaf

black pepper

1$\frac{1}{4}$tsp salt

1 egg well beaten

1 cup grated cheese, Parmesan for preference

$\frac{1}{2}$ cup ($\frac{1}{4}$pt) olive oil

For the sauce:

$\frac{1}{2}$ cup chopped onion mixed with chopped shallot and garlic

2$\frac{1}{2}$ cups tomatoes, peeled and sliced (preserved, frozen,

tinned tomatoes and purée can be used)

1tsp salt

black pepper

1tsp chopped basil

To make the polenta squares, bring milk to boil with the bay leaf, salt and pepper. Gradually stir in the polenta. Turn down the heat or even remove the milk from it when you do this and stir quickly and constantly because it thickens quickly. Simmer for 3min stirring all the time. Remove from the heat. Add the beaten egg, blending it in well. Combine half the cheese and half the olive oil with this mixture. Turn it into an oiled baking tin about 1$\frac{1}{2}$in deep. Smooth it out, cool and then cut into 2in squares. Arrange these in a shallow baking dish.

Make the sauce by first melting the onion mixture in a little of the oil. Add the tomatoes and the rest of the oil and simmer for 5min. Add half the basil and the seasoning. Pour the sauce around the polenta squares and sprinkle the remaining cheese over them. Bake in a hot oven, 400° F, 205° C for 30min. Sprinkle on the rest of the basil just before serving.

This is a good party starter if you have many guests, for it can be prepared well in advance.

BEANS

Growing

Climbing beans can be fitted into almost any garden. Even those who have no garden at all can grow them up the side of a door or around a window. They do well as a screen on a balcony and as a covering for a backyard wall, especially if this is whitewashed, so that the contrast of red and green is effective. They look attractive neatly and inexpensively trained up a tripod of bamboos at the back of a flower border. You can nip out their tips when they have grown as high as you want them. Scarlet runners have red and pink flowers, Blue Coco mauve, and The Czar white flowers. All are continuously in bloom until autumn.

Do not think that it is essential to have a bean row—two rows of stout staves lashed to horizontal poles tied at the point where they cross. This can be expensive in materials and time. Use instead a 'Maypole', a strong central pole with strings radiating from its top and pegged into the soil with wires. Plant a bean to each string. This type of wigwam support is much easier to erect.

All beans need a rich, well-manured yet light soil, although late sowing of broad beans can be made on a moister, slightly heavier loam, in which case watch out for slugs.

French beans need an open sunny site, and runners too, although these will tolerate partial shade. Early crops of broad beans do best on a south-facing border. Later crops can go in the open garden.

Sow broad beans from February to April in mild districts and a month later elsewhere. Sown in November in mild areas, they stand the winter and crop early.

Sow French beans from the end of April to the end of July, runners during the first week in May. Make drills 3in deep. Alternatively dibble the seeds in using a line as a guide.

If the weather is dry, soak the seed drills before sowing or sometimes it is best instead to soak the seeds for an hour first.

Keep the rows of young plants well mulched with manure, garden compost or lawn mowings. Water freely in dry weather. Runner-bean flowers fall off in drought conditions. As soon as the pods form give liquid fertilisers.

Pick all kinds young, they take less time to cook and taste much better. You can grow dual-purpose crops and pick some of the 'dryers' while they are young for fresh vegetables and leave those that follow to mature.

Let these become quite ripe and then pull up the entire plant. Hang it upside down in a dry, airy place. Remember, the pod is sterile inside. If you shell beans too early they will go mouldy in store. Wait until the pods are quite dry and the beans fall easily from them. Store in bags or jars.

Cooking broad beans

These are the earliest to mature. If you grow any type other than the modern dwarf varieties, which need no support, you should pinch out the tips of the stems when the first flowers open. You can cook these tips like spinach.

For the most delicious flavour of all, cook whole broad beans, just 2in long, gathered as soon as the petals have faded from them.

Otherwise, gather the pods when the beans are not much larger than a good-sized pea. Try them à la croque-au-sel, raw with salt, as a savoury when you are having guests in for a casual drink. Let your guests shell them as they eat, but the beans must be both young and freshly picked.

The tough outer coat on old beans is very indigestible to some people. To cook old beans boil in boiling salted water for approximately 20min, cool under cold water, slip the beans from the skins and reheat in a little butter. Alternatively, skin and make a purée of them.

Parsley is a herb often used with broad beans although sage gives them more flavour. However, savory is the best herb for broad beans. Whichever one you use, boil the beans with a sprig or two and add more, chopped finely, to the strained beans.

Cooking French beans

The haricots verts of the restaurant menus must be one of the most easily prepared of all vegetables. Simply top and tail and wash.

Usually, once they are ready you can gather French beans every day, so it is as well to have more than one way of serving them. If you can gather only a few at a time, they store well unprepared in a refrigerator in a plastic bag or food container.

These beans are quite delicious simply boiled fairly fast in enough salted boiling water to cover them. If they are young they will be tender in only a few minutes.

From this step you can take them further to make many fine dishes. They can also be served cold as a salad in a variety of dressings. Hot, they can be served or mixed with melted butter, cream, eggs, tomato, bacon, wine, gravy and many other sauces. Try them cooked with onions and slightly browned in the following dish.

French Beans à la Lyonnaise (serves 4)

1lb freshly boiled beans	a little salt and pepper
6oz finely sliced onions	lemon juice
1oz butter	finely chopped parsley

Fry the onions in half the butter until lightly browned. Add the rest of the butter and the seasoning. Lightly stir in the beans and fry all these gently together until the beans too are slightly browned. Take out with a draining spoon, place in a warm dish and keep hot while you add the lemon juice to the pan and with a wooden spoon remove all the brown from the base and sides. If necessary, moisten with a little of the water the beans were boiled in but do not make it too wet. Pour this over the beans and sprinkle them with the parsley.

Cooking runner beans

Many people like runners sliced as finely as possible, but I prefer them snapped, American-style, and this is much quicker. I think that the thicker sections have a better flavour than the slices, which seem to lose so much to the water they are boiled in. After stringing the beans (a potato peeler does this very quickly and efficiently) simply snap them into roughly 1in lengths.

Salted Runner Beans for Winter Use

For years I salted runner beans for winter use and very enjoyable they were! You can use either 1gal jars or 2lb and 3lb jars for storing the beans and I found the last the most convenient. On the days when I had not enough beans to fill the small jars I simply finished with a layer of salt and covered the jar and stood it in a cool place until the next day. Inevitably, the level drops, so it is always wise to top it up a day later. Beginning with a layer of salt $\frac{1}{2}$–1in deep, add a 2in layer of sliced beans and then more salt, deep enough to hide all traces of the beans below. Continue making alternate layers of salt and beans, finishing with a top layer of salt. To use, take them from the salt early in the morning, soak in fresh cold water and keep changing this until you can taste that it is no longer salty. Cook the beans without salt but with an onion to give them a good colour.

Runner Bean Casserole (serves 4)

1lb runner beans
1 hearted lettuce or a good
   handful of thinnings
salt, paprika

4 medium green onions (with
   their tops)
2oz butter

For the topping, which is optional:

1 cup white breadcrumbs, to
   which you can add if you
   wish
2tbsp melted bacon dripping or
   butter

1tbsp finely chopped bacon
   and/or chopped nuts
parsley for garnish

Shred the lettuce finely. Chop the onions and slice the tops finely. Butter an oven dish and fill it with alternate layers of vegetables with the sliced or snapped beans at the bottom and the top. Sprinkle a little salt and paprika over each layer and dot it with butter. Dot the top layer well with butter and cover the dish. Bake it in a moderate oven for 1hr, longer if the oven is used at a lower temperature or if you have to open it from time to time. This dish will keep warm while others are made ready for serving.

To make the topping, fry the breadcrumbs in the melted fat and when they are nicely golden add the bacon and/or nuts. Sprinkle this over the top of the vegetables just before serving and garnish with chopped parsley.

Cooking haricot beans

In many other countries different varieties of dwarf beans are shelled and cooked in the same way as peas and are eaten fresh as well as dried. They are then known as flageolets. They are delicious eaten like peas with lamb, but they should be cooked with a bouquet garni and not mint.

You can vary ways of serving them. They are fine tossed in butter with chopped herbs, slightly browned with onions like the French beans or boiled with bacon—put them in 15min before the bacon is ready to lift out. They can be served cold in a variety of dressings as a filling salad.

Fresh Haricot Bean Salad (serves 4)

1qt fresh shelled beans, any
colour
2 small green onions
1 shallot with green top
bouquet garni of sprig of
thyme, small sprig sage, bay

leaf, tied with the shallot and
onion tops
French dressing
2tbsp mixed chopped chives,
chervil and parsley

Boil the beans in salted boiling water with the bouquet garni, the shallot and one onion until tender, about 15min. Slice the other onion finely. Drain the beans well, remove onion, shallot and bouquet garni. While they are still warm, mix them with the sliced onion and the dressing. Add herbs. Taste, add milled pepper to suit. Allow to cool. Serve on crisp lettuce leaves.

Cooking dried haricots
I never soak beans for long because this can cause them to begin fermenting and so become indigestible, as well as taking away some of their delicate flavour. An hour, sufficient to make them begin to swell, is enough.

A pressure cooker saves cooking time. Otherwise, put the beans in plenty of cold water, bring them to the boil, skim off the scum that usually appears at first, and then season. If you add salt earlier they will take much longer to become soft.

These beans are always more tasty when some aromatic vegetables such as garlic, an onion stuck with cloves, a bay leaf, parsnip, carrot or Hamburg parsley, basil or a bouquet garni are cooked with them. One flavour enhances the other. At the end you also have some pleasantly flavoured liquor as a base for soup.

Some people like to cook a little bacon or pork fat with the beans. This is a good way to use a knuckle, trotter, a piece of salt pork or even some pork skin.

If you have a freezer
Freeze the beans in 1lb quantities. Allow a little headroom for all kinds. Broad beans: small, blanch 2min; medium, 3min; old, first shell, then 4min. Haricots fresh, blanch 2min. Runners, snap or slice, 3min. French, top and tail only, 3min.

BEETROOTS

Growing

Sandy soil, well manured for some previous crop, grows the best beet-roots. If you have heavy soil try to keep it light and open with plenty of humus and peat.

There are globe, cylindrical and long beetroots. I grow the first two because they occupy less garden space for less time than the long kind.

Sow beetroot in April and then in succession until the end of May. The long type should be sown in mid-May and lifted in November and stored through the winter in dry sand or peat in a cool, dark shed. 1oz of seed will sow 25ft. Drills should be 1in deep, the rows 12–15in apart. Sow radishes between the rows to save wasting space in early days.

If the ruddy coloration of beetroot when mixed with other vegetables irritates you, you may like to know that there is now a white variety, Snowhite. Its leaves are green and, like the others, can be cooked. The flesh is full flavoured. Golden beet has a yellow-orange flesh. This too does not colour other foods and its tops are green.

One of the most useful beets is the leaf type or Spinach beet. Another variety, Swiss chard, has a dual crop. This is sometimes called silver seakale beet, a reference to its thick stems or midribs, the chards.

On good soil the leaves grow very large and you may find that a dozen plants is enough for a family of two or three. I grow more, a 20ft row, and freeze the 'spinach'.

This also should be sown in April in slightly deeper drills and in rows 18in apart. If the plants are kept well cut and the rows covered with a cloche in late autumn you can gather them all through winter and on until sowing time comes around again.

Cooking

About 15min in boiling salted water will cook beetroot if you pull the plants when they are young. They should be sweet and tender enough to be eaten grated raw in salads.

They can also be baked in a hot oven. Wash them well, scrubbing them gently with a soft brush to remove all traces of soil. Place them on a dish and bake until they are soft to the touch, about 30min.

Cook beetroots as a vegetable, served hot with lamb and mint sauce. Cook them whole and serve with a hot cheese sauce laced with nutmeg. Skin under slow running cold water and reheat in a little butter.

When globe roots are ready they should be smaller than a tennis ball. I like to deal with a whole row at a time, thus releasing the ground for another crop. This is optional, of course, but it suits my way of gardening.

Every part of the plant can be cooked and/or frozen. First, cut off all the leaves at about ½in above the crown. Next remove their stalks and set these on one side for soup. Wash the leaves thoroughly and cook or freeze as for spinach. They become greener when cooked. Save the water to cook the stems, peels and crowns together later. Wash the stems well, make into little bundles and cut through in fine sections. They can then be cooked and puréed to make a delicious borsch soup which can be frozen if required.

Russian Borsch

1 cup (½pt) each peeled and diced beetroot, carrot, onion	1 cup my beetroot purée
1tbsp butter	1 cup finely shredded cabbage
2 cups (1pt) good stock—beef is best	1tbsp lemon juice
	sour cream

Begin with diced vegetables, cover them with cold water, put on lid, simmer for 20min. Add butter, stock, purée and cabbage. Stir well and bring to boil. Add lemon juice. Serve. After ladling the soup into bowls put in each dish 1tbsp thick sour cream which should have been kept at room temperature to prevent it chilling the soup.

Beetroot in Citrus Sauce (serves 4)

This is good with baked ham and duck. I find it best to use one of the earthenware saucepans for this rather than a double boiler.

2 cups diced beetroot	alternatively mild cider vinegar)
3tbsp brown sugar	
1tbsp cornflour	2oz butter
½tsp salt	1tbsp marmalade
½ cup dry white wine (or any good home-made kind, or	4tbsp cream

Put all but the beetroot, marmalade and cream in the pan and cook, stirring frequently, until all are blended and the liquid clear. Add the beetroot and marmalade. Let the mixture continue to simmer very gently, just moving, but do not let it boil. Add the butter, and when this is blended add the cream and serve. Takes less than an hour.

Cooking leaf beets, Swiss chard

Usually the leaves and stalks are cooked and served separately. Strip the green from the white stems, which should be cut close to the ground, by running a knife down each side. Sometimes the stalks or chards are so large that they must be divided. Cooked in boiling salted water alone they become discoloured and unattractive, but a slice of lemon, a squeeze of juice or even a dash of vinegar will keep them beautifully white. Drain well and serve hot with melted butter.

The boiled chards are also good with a thick tomato sauce and grated cheese. Do not overcook or they may become fibrous— 10–15min is enough.

To serve the chards as a vegetable with either meat or fish—it is one of the few greens that go well with fish—serve with melted butter or margarine and a generous sprinkling of fresh chervil or green fennel.

To cook all kinds of spinach use only the water adhering to the leaves after washing. Be sure to wash in several waters to remove all soil. Put them with either a lump of butter or 1tbsp olive oil and 1tsp salt in a heavy pan. Bring slowly to the boil. After 5min turn top to bottom so that the leaves cook evenly. When tender, about 10min, strain and chop.

If you have a freezer

Get the most out of the crop of Swiss chard by freezing the green spinach part, and eating the chards while they are fresh. These will not freeze. If you have a surefeit, cut the stems into thin slices and use for soup. Once boiled they are easily creamed in a blender. Use garlic and shallot to flavour the purée, and blend these too. All you have to do to complete the soup is to dilute to the thickness you like and season. A little cream improves both texture and appearance.

I freeze the leaves of all beet, ie, Swiss chard, spinach beet, beet leaves, in 1lb lots, blanching them for 2min and then packing them in plastic containers with a little headroom.

To freeze the beetroots, cook them as usual, then cool, skin, and slice. Pack them in bags or cartons and freeze.

Once thawed they are ready to serve cold. To serve hot, heat in butter or margarine.

BLACKBERRIES

Growing

For the little space it demands for its roots a blackberry plant gives tremendous value, but although it takes only a little room in the soil it needs a good area for its top growth or canes. Even so it can be an economical plant, for it can be trained on a sunny fence, along boundary wires or against a building such as a shed or garage, thus adding space to your garden plot. If no such space is available if can be grown and trained horizontally along wires placed one above the other at, say, 12in spacing, at the side of a path or at the end of a garden, or it can be used as a screen in some useful place.

Modern hybrids give large yields. Usually one plant is enough for a small family. Furthermore, if this is a consideration, you can have thornless types. According to variety you can have fruits in late July and August through to October. If you have a freezer in which the freshly picked fruit can be stored, the times of fruiting may not be of great significance to you, but if you have to take holidays in August, for example, a late cropper may be your best choice.

Cultivation is very simple. Blackberries like deep, rich, moist loam. Poor soil should be prepared and enriched before planting and then continually top dressed. Plant the canes in autumn. After they have fruited, cut away the productive shoots to ground level and begin tying and training the new shoots as soon as this is possible. Fan them out in such a way that they spring freely from the ground and do not cross each other as they grow.

Each winter, top dress the plants with well-decayed animal manure or home-made compost.

Loganberries are grown in the same way as blackberries and can be substituted for raspberries in any recipe.

Cooking

I like to cast a cupful or so of raw blackberries over a fruit salad. If you plan to make bramble jelly with them, always include a few red, unripe berries because these provide pectin and help the jelly to set more quickly.

Spiced Bramble Jelly

This jelly has the advantage that it can be served with cheese as a pickle as well as with scones and cream in the more usual way. Follow the same recipe but omit the spices if you want plain bramble jelly.

Weigh the fruit. For each 1lb use 1tsp mixed spice. Wash the fruit and put it with the spice in a covered heatproof dish in a slow oven. Bake until the fruits are tender and begin to exude juice freely. Put all in a jelly bag and let it drip all night. Make sure that all the juice is drawn off by squeezing the bag should this appear necessary. Measure the juice. Use a preserving pan and allow 1lb sugar to 1pt juice. Warm the sugar, add it to the juice, stir until dissolved, bring the liquid to the boil and let it boil rapidly until it gels. Have the jars warming in the oven. Pour in the jelly. Let it cool and then cover the jars.

Blackberry Sorbet

This is one of the quickest sorbets to make and is especially useful if you have a store of blackberry juice already strained. To extract the juice, put the berries in a covered casserole dish and gently bake them in a slow oven until you can see that the juice is running freely. Pour this into a jelly bag and let it drip into a bowl all night.

| 1pt juice | ½oz powdered gelatine |
| 3tbsp sugar | 1 egg white |

Heat sugar and juice together but try not to boil it too long. Dissolve the gelatine in 1tbsp water and add this to the liquid. Stir until all is dissolved and then allow to cool. When almost firm beat it well to make it fluffy. I use the electric mixer for this. Beat the egg white and add this to the blackberry mixture. Freeze.

Blackberry Wine

6lb blackberries　　　　**4lb sugar**
1 lemon　　　　　　　　**wine yeast**
1gal boiling water

Peel the lemon thinly with a potato peeler. Put the rind and the blackberries into a large bowl or plastic bucket and pour the gallon of boiling water over them. Allow to stand, covered, for 3 days. Stir daily. Have the sugar ready in another bucket. Strain the berries on to it. Stir well. Add the lemon juice. Mix the yeast with a little of the liquid made lukewarm and add this to the bulk. (Remember to activate the yeast 2 days in advance.) Cover and leave for 24hr in a warm place. Pour all into a fermenting jar and insert an air lock. Bottle the wine after all fermentation has ceased. It is not possible to give the exact length of this period, it might be several months, depending on the temperature of the home, but do be patient for it is most unwise to hurry.

If you have a freezer
Wash and drain the fruit thoroughly. Pack it into bags or cartons.

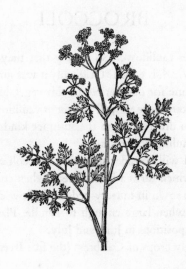

BORAGE

Growing

This is an easily grown annual with lovely blue flowers. Once you have it in your garden you can expect it to seed itself and to reappear each year. It grows to some 1–2ft, has slightly hairy leaves and a grey, misty appearance. It will grow well in any ordinary soil. Sow the seeds outdoors in March for June and July flowers, and in September to stand the winter and produce May flowers.

Cooking

Press the leaves or stem between finger and thumb and you will notice a distinct cucumber perfume which makes the herb a welcome ingredient for summer salads, but for this purpose use only young and tender leaves.

Sprigs of the stems bearing flowers and mixed with sprigs of mint can be used to garnish many kinds of iced drinks, especially fruit cups. Borage is also used in claret cup.

The individual flowers can be used to garnish salads and sweets. They look charming, for instance, on whipped cream. The flowers can also be candied.

Leaves can be dipped in batter and fried, well drained and served as a sweet, sprinkled with vanilla sugar.

BROCCOLI

Growing

Broccoli resembles cauliflowers so closely that they almost seem indistinguishable. Which is which? Originally it was simply that broccoli was the Italian name for one variety of this vegetable, which we imported out of season. Now we call all winter cauliflowers broccoli. As these are really no different from the summer kinds I will deal with them under the cauliflower heading.

In this section I will consider sprouting broccoli only. This can be green or purple which turns a lovely green when cooked.

Seeds should be sown in nursery beds in shallow drills in April and May. Transplant when large enough to handle. Plant 2ft apart each way in their final positions in June and July.

If you want early crops of Calabrese (the fine freezing variety) sow under glass in February and plant out in May, otherwise sow at the same time as the rest.

Cooking

The shoots should be whole and firm after cooking, yet tender and succulent. Never overcook or you will spoil their attractive appearance. Melted butter is one of the best accompaniments. However, this vegetable is fine enough to be served as a first course, in which case a choice sauce, such as Hollandaise, makes it a special dish.

Place the shoots with the stems all going the same way in boiling salted water, its level about ½in above them. Cover the pan, bring again to the boil and boil gently for about 10min. Turn off the heat and leave them in the covered pan for 5min longer. Drain by lifting them out with a fish slice; this prevents the shoots from being broken.

When you gather the shoots take the whole stem back to the main stem and cut with a knife at this point. Should the shoot's lower stem seem tough, peel that portion before cooking.

Broccoli leaves can be cooked like any other greens. Those at the tips of the plant will be more tender than those at the base. Boil them with a small onion and a lump of sugar or a little honey to eliminate any too strong brassica flavour.

I find that the small shoots produced by the plant towards the end of the crop make a fine and unusual chilled soup. I boil them as usual, blend them with their water to make a purée, season, add a beaten egg and a little cream and finally serve with chopped fresh herbs after chilling well.

BRUSSELS SPROUTS

Growing

I like to sow Brussels sprouts outdoors early in the season, in March. This gives me sprouts from November to April. If you want them earlier you can sow seed in boxes in a greenhouse, frame, or under a cloche in January or February.

Brussels must be transplanted early so that they receive no check. Sow them thinly in a nursery bed and prick them out early. They should be in their final positions in late May or June. They must be planted in firm ground or they will not form tight sprouts.

I grow those varieties which produce a medium sprout and I gather these small, not much bigger than a large hazelnut. They need little preparation, maybe an outer leaf or two taken off, but that is all. Such varieties do not take much room—plant them 2ft apart all ways. Furthermore, their leaves are not so gross as the larger varieties and are good and tender when cooked.

The tops of Brussels should not be cut until all the sprouts have been harvested. They are then 'spring greens'. I like to begin with these tops and then, if I am not in a hurry to clear the crop, to work my way down the denuded stem, taking three leaves from each plant until the tough old ones are reached. The plants are then pulled up. These leaves are beautifully tender and by using them you prolong the value of your crop. Alternatively you can gather the leaves down the stem as you gather the sprouts. If you pull them off as you go you will find it easier to pick the sprouts. Cook the leaves separately as you would broccoli.

In some seasons the sprouts begin to elongate. They are still good to eat.

Cooking
If, like me, you enjoy beautifully green, firm yet tender sprouts, use small ones. Wash well and boil them in just enough water to float them. Measure this and bring it to the boil after adding a small onion cut into four and enough salt to suit your taste.

Put in the sprouts, cover and boil slowly for 10min. Turn off the heat and let the covered pan stand on the cooling ring for another 5min before straining and serving.

Any left-over sprouts can be covered with French dressing and a good sprinkling of nutmeg to make a good salad. They mix well with nuts. I particularly enjoy cold sprouts with walnuts.

If you have a freezer
I find that I tend to freeze just a pound or two at a time as they are ready. Always gather more than you want and do half for the pot and half for the freezer. Blanch small sprouts for 3min and medium ones for 4min. Leave a little headroom.

C

CABBAGE

Growing

You can have cabbages the year round. Winter varieties differ slightly, are often tinged purple and are hardier than those of spring and summer. Included in winter types are savoys, which have curlier leaves of a slightly different texture and flavour than cabbage. Some of the spring varieties are pointed in shape. Modern varieties of summer and autumn cabbage are ideal for small gardens, compact, rock-hard and 'long-standing', by which we mean that they remain in good condition for many weeks and do not bolt, that is, run quickly from heart to flower stem, as so many of the old varieties do.

Cabbages have long-lasting qualities when cut. One variety, Winter Keeper, ready for cutting in October and November onwards, can be stored in a cool, airy shed and will remain in good condition for weeks. Pull up the entire stem for storing and hang upside down.

For summer and autumn use, the seed should be sown in March and April in shallow drills in seed beds, and planted out in June and July. For early summer crops sow seeds in a cold frame in January. Spring cabbage should be sown in July and August and planted out in September and October. Red cabbage can be sown both in spring and summer.

Cooking

First a word about red cabbage. This is an easily grown vegetable which helps you to give an exotic touch to your menus. Use it for poultry; it is delicious with Christmas goose, game, sausages, gammon steaks and as a main supper dish with chestnuts. It is best cooked in a covered casserole. First shred it. Melt 1tbsp bacon dripping or butter in the casserole. Season it with a little salt, pepper, 1tsp vinegar or a little red wine or cider. Add cabbage and stir well. Cover and cook in a moderate oven or on the stove in a gentle heat. Cooking time is about 2hr, so it can go in with the joint.

To provide a variety, when it is three-quarters cooked add apples—two cookers to a medium sized head—peeled and quartered, with 1tbsp brown sugar.

Red Cabbage and Chestnuts (serves 4)

Everyone who has eaten this with me has asked for the recipe. It is substantial enough for a supper dish. It is also rich enough for Christmas. It may also be used as a stuffing for large onions, marrow rings and green peppers. I have made this dish successfully with large butter beans as a substitute for the nuts. If you do this, watch that you do not overcook them.

1 medium sized red cabbage or half a large one	1 cup ($\frac{1}{2}$pt) peeled chestnuts
	2tbsp sugar
$\frac{1}{2}$ cup white wine or vinegar (I like cider vinegar for this dish)	2oz seedless raisins
	2oz butter or good bacon dripping
1 large cooking apple peeled and sliced	salt, paprika
	1tbsp flour
	1tbsp sherry or good white wine

Shred the cabbage finely and put it into a bowl, cover with boiling water and one half the white wine or vinegar. Let this soak for 15min. Meanwhile prepare the apples and chestnuts. Bring them to the boil with $\frac{1}{2}$pt water, sugar, the rest of the wine or vinegar and the raisins. Simmer until tender. Drain the cabbage thoroughly. Heat the fat and put in the cabbage with a good sprinkling of salt and paprika. Stir it around until all is coated with the fat and very slightly browned (10-15min). Cover the pan and let all simmer for 10min.

Sprinkle the flour over the cabbage. Stir well. Add the chestnut mixture. Blend. Taste and adjust seasoning. Add sherry and serve.

Cabbage for Salad

Modern varieties of cabbage are perfect for shredding or grating and a cabbage salad in the middle of the lettuce season makes a nice change. However, it is in winter that they give us greatest value as a salad crop. A mixture of red and white cabbage is both attractive and tasty. If you want a pretty table decoration use a red cabbage as a salad bowl. Remove the heart, wash the outer leaves. Stand in a shallow dish or bowl and fill with the mixed salad.

Cabbage Stalks and Stumps

Most people remove these and throw them away. We used to love to eat them raw as children. To cook, peel away the tough outer fibrous skin until only the tender inner portion remains. Cut this into slices or cubes. Boil these in enough water just to cover them. Take 1tbsp bacon dripping or butter to which is added a small chopped onion, a shallot and a clove of garlic. Cover and melt over a low heat until these are soft but not browned. Remove from heat, add 1tbsp flour, stir and, when all are blended, pour in the water from the cabbage stumps. Stir until it thickens. Add the cooked stumps etc, and a good dash of nutmeg. (This is a fine spice to use with all brassica dishes.)

If you want to make it richer, add a little cream or beat in an egg, but do not boil it after this or the egg will curdle. Use this vegetable with a main dish. An excellent first-course dish can be made by dividing the mixture into individual ramekins, adding chopped crisp bacon and sprinkling with buttered breadcrumbs or grated cheese. Grill before serving.

Cabbage Bread

If you bake your own bread, try cabbage bread for a change. I think that you will enjoy it.

Make the dough in the usual way. Cut a piece for the loaf and let it rise as usual. Have ready a large, clean cabbage leaf. Before putting the dough in the oven wrap the leaf around it. Place it on the dough in such a way that its centre vein runs along the centre of the loaf. When the bread is baked it becomes imprinted with the vein and leaf pattern. Surprisingly, the cabbage gives the bread a delicious, spicy flavour.

If you have a freezer

I cannot understand why we are so often told that cabbage does not freeze well. Perhaps it doesn't as pure cabbage, but here is how I freeze quantities each year, a useful thing to know if you want to clear a row in the garden.

Cut each head into four and remove the thickest part of the stalk. Add a peeled onion and a peeled, cored apple, both quartered. Cook together in just a little unsalted boiling water for 5min. Drain the mixture and place in a container leaving a little headroom and freeze.

To use, add salt to a very little water, put the frozen block and a knob of butter and cook in a covered pan, cook until tender usually about 10min after it comes to the boil.

Red cabbage and red-cabbage dishes also freeze well. Cook first reheat when required. I usually prepare the cabbage for Christmas in advance and freeze it, for this saves a lot of time on the day.

Growing Chinese cabbage

If you like Chinese cooking you really ought to grow this vegetable because it features in so many dishes. Botanically it is a brassica, a member of the cabbage tribe. It is known as Petsai and there are varieties such as Mi-Chihili, Wongbok and a new F1 hybrid, Wonder Cross. The long leaves have wavy, crisp margins. The hearts grow long, resembling a cos lettuce.

This is one of the several vegetables to be sown in summer, late July.

It is important that the crop grows fast and well, otherwise the plants may be small and tough. The soil needs to be light and open, but with a porosity given by much well-rotted manure and humus and not by starvation. Make the drills 2in deep, water them and sprinkle in 1in peat. Water this. Sow the seed very thinly and as soon as you can see that they are growing well, thin out the seedlings to 9in apart. Keep watering—there are likely to be some hot days and the combination of water and warmth will keep the plants growing.

I like to put grass mowings down between rows of vegetables of this kind. These generate considerable heat. I often line deep drills with them and cover them with peat and soil when I sow marrows, sweet corn or beans in late spring. They provide useful humus in time. Keep them 1in or so away from the plant itself. Lay the grass on quite deep and scatter a few slug pellets about as well.

Cooking Chinese cabbage
You can treat this vegetable like a lettuce or a salad cabbage and you can also cook it in the same way as cabbage. Strip off the soft green part of the leaves and cook these like spinach and the thick midribs like seakale. You can also eat these stems like celery. The roots can be used, peeled and sliced, in soups. The Chinese method is to sauté or 'stir-fry' the shredded leaves in vegetable oil.

Allspice is a good seasoning for this vegetable..

Fried Slices of Lamb with Vegetables

This is a Chinese recipe.

½lb lean lamb, a fillet from the
    leg is best
oil for frying
4oz onions
1oz mushrooms
1oz cucumber
4oz bamboo shoots (I buy a
    large tin and deep freeze the
    remainder when I have taken
    what is needed here)

1lb Chinese cabbage, white
few drops sesame oil
white stock
1tsp sugar
salt, pepper
soy sauce
1tsp cornflour

Slice the meat and vegetables finely, shred the cabbage. Mix the cornflour in a little of the stock.

Put a little oil and salt in the pan. Heat and fry everything but the meat for a few minutes, turning them well. Add the meat, pepper, sesame oil and a little stock. Cook a minute longer. Add the sugar, a few drops of soy sauce and the stock. Stir. Wait until the stock boils. Add the cornflour. Stir until it thickens and then serve.

CARROTS

Growing
You can grow carrots the year round, using frames and cloches to protect early crops. Some varieties are better for forcing than others and these are clearly marked in seedsmen's catalogues.

This crop does best on deep, well-cultivated soil. Freshly manured land results in branching, fibrous roots, so select a site which was manured earlier for some previous crop.

Sow the forcing kinds under cloches or in frames from January to March. You can sow in the open ground from early March, but only if the ground is warm and dry, otherwise wait until April. Main crops are sown from April to June and you can sow them in succession. Drills should be just about ¾in deep and 9in apart. Thin as soon as the true leaves appear.

I like to go along the row several times, first thinning out to only about 1in apart. The plants are then left until their crowns are touching and then I pull alternate roots and leave the others to swell, and I repeat this until the crop is cleared. Often when they are about 4in apart I leave them to mature as main crops to use in winter. These should be lifted in October and stored in layers in bins of dry earth, peat or sand in a shed or cellar.

Cooking

For the maximum flavour cook them this way. Wash and scrub but do not peel. Cook in just enough boiling salted water to cover them, simmering them until they have absorbed all the water. Remove from the pan and peel. Melt a little butter in the pan, return the carrots and gently warm them through in the butter. Sprinkle with chopped parsley and serve.

Glazed Carrots

These are delicious served with a roast joint such as veal or pork.

Scrub the carrots well and boil them in their skins in just enough boiling salted water to cover them until they are tender. Skin and halve them. Coat them in melted butter and sprinkle them with brown sugar, a little salt and a dusting of paprika. Heat them in a large, heavy pan over a low heat. Shake them so that you keep them well basted with the melted butter and sugar until they are glazed.

Sweet Carrots

Carrots can be used as a sweet by cutting glazed carrots into rings to fill a flan. Sprinkle with extra sugar or spread with honey.

Carrot Jam

This is really intended to be used quickly, otherwise you must include brandy, which makes it a little expensive—but exclusive! Decorate individual tarts with a blob of cream and a little angelica.

First stew the carrots, drain, and either put them in an electric blender or sieve them. To 1lb pulp add 1lb preserving sugar, the grated rind of 1 lemon and the juice of 2 lemons. If you are using brandy you will need 2tbsp.

Boil the sugar and the pulp together for 5min. Skim if necessary. Add the lemon juice and rind. Stir well and remove from heat. Stir in the brandy if this is used. Pour into hot pots. Tie or close to make the jars airtight.

Carrot Wine

6lb carrots	rind and juice of 1 lemon and
1gal water	1 orange
4lb white sugar	yeast
1lb wheat (obtainable from a health store)	4oz raisins

Scrub and slice carrots. Boil them until tender in 1gal water. Strain the liquid into a bucket over the sugar, wheat and citrus rinds. Stir well. When it is lukewarm add fruit juices, raisins and prepared yeast. Stir well and leave to ferment for 7 days, stirring daily. Remove rinds but not raisins. Pour all into fermentation jar with airlock. Bottle when all fermentation has ceased.

If you have a freezer
I freeze only whole baby carrots because the old ones store so well. Carrots can be kept frozen for 12 months. Scrub or peel and blanch for 5min for whole carrots; diced, sliced or cut into strips, blanch for 2min.

CAULIFLOWER

Growing

For a small garden, All the Year Round is a good variety and it can be sown at all seasons. There are others, both summer and winter kinds. The latter, usually called broccoli, comes into season from October until April, according to variety. It is best to decide just when you want to gather the heads and work back from there.

For summer use you can sow seeds indoors in gentle heat in February and March. Harden off the plants before they go out into the garden. For the main crop sow outdoors from March to May according to variety in drills ¾in deep in rows on a nursery bed. Sow, thin out and finally prick out to 4in apart each way. Plant them into their final positions as soon as possible in June and July.

Essentials are a well-limed soil, even in the nursery-bed stage. Heavy, yet well-drained soil, manured for some previous crop, suts them best. Freshly manured, light soil will not produce good tight heads and firm curds.

Cooking

I like to cook a cauliflower whole in a saucepan deep enough to take it standing head up. I use boiling salted water and let it come almost to the top of the head. Cover the pan. When the main stalk is just tender the curds are cooked enough.

From this point there are all kinds of nice things you can do, from simply pouring melted butter over to cooking it au gratin.

If you like contrasts of textures, fry 2 heaped tbsp breadcrumbs in 3tbsp butter until they are golden brown. Pour these over the cauliflower when you serve it and at the same time sprinkle finely chopped chervil or parsley over it also. It will look good and taste delicious.

Cauliflower leaves should be cooked and not thrown away. One good way to do them is to shred them, including the thick midrib. Cook them in just enough water to float them with salt and a little butter. Let them simmer until tender.

So don't get too carried away by that lovely creamy curd; remember that all other parts of this vegetable can be eaten, even the thick stalks. Cut these across and use them for cream of cauliflower soup. You can peel thick stems, stumps and ribs and use them in the same way as described for cabbage stumps.

Cauliflower lends itself to other methods of cooking than boiling or steaming. It is good baked and fried.

Fried Cauliflower

Cook, drain and separate a head of cauliflower into individual florets each about 1in across.

For the batter:

2 eggs yolks	$\frac{3}{4}$ cup of flour
$\frac{1}{2}$ cup milk	pinch salt

Beat the eggs and milk together. Stir the mixture into the flour and salt. Beat until smooth. Let it stand for 1hr, covered.

Meanwhile soak the cauliflower sprigs in a little oil and vinegar, 2 parts olive oil to 1 part vinegar, or alternatively, lemon juice. Drain them after $\frac{1}{2}$hr. When ready to cook, dip each sprig into the batter and fry in deep fat. Drain well. Garnish with sprigs of fried parsley. Serve with an aromatic tomato sauce.

If you have a freezer
Freeze as directed for broccoli. This vegetable often becomes an embarrassment since all plants tend to come into maturity at the same time. A freezer solves ensuing problems.

CELERIAC

Growing
The important thing is to sow the seeds early, in March, indoors in heat. Prick the seedlings out into boxes as soon as you can handle them. Keep them indoors but begin hardening them off in late April and plant out in June, 18in between the plants, 12in apart in rows. The soil needs to be light and rich and the site sunny.

Keep all the side shoots removed as they form so that you have just one main topknot of leaves. In August begin drawing up a little soil around the base of the plant and continue to do this as the root swells.

Be sure to water them well in dry weather. Lift roots at the end of

October and twist off the leaves. Store in dry sand or peat, alternatively, leave in the ground and lift when required.

Cooking

All recipes for celery can be applied to the turnip-rooted celeriac. The texture differs but the flavour is much the same. Indeed, I think that it is often better in the root vegetable. Celeriac can be shredded or grated and eaten raw in sandwiches and as a salad. It is delicious in any creamy or yogurt-based sauces. When cooked its texture resembles parsnips more than stalk celery.

Stuffed Celeriac Rings

2 large celeriac roots	butter
carrot	grated cheese
onion	nutmeg

You will see why I haven't given the exact measurements for the carrot and onion in a moment. Pare the roots of celeriac and cut them through into 1in thick slices. Add to boiling salted water and boil for 5min. Take out and cool. Trim each to make a good shape and equal rounds. In the centre of each ring scoop out a hollow almost to the

depth of the slice and for about half its diameter. Save the scoopings and trimmings. Chop this pulp finely and weigh or measure it. Prepare an equal quantity of onion and carrot, half of each, finely chopped. Melt these with butter in a pan until they are soft but not browned. Mix all with the chopped celeriac. Divide the mixture equally among the rings, filling the hollows and raising them a little.

Place the rings on a buttered oven dish. Cover them with finely grated cheese—Parmesan is best. Sprinkle with a little nutmeg and bake in a moderate oven until brown, about 1hr.

If you have a freezer
You can freeze rings like those described above as well as diced and sliced celeriac. Peel and blanch for 2min. Pack, leaving a little head-room.

CELERY

Growing
If you grow celery the traditional way, the preparation for the crop can prove to be very hard work. However, there are some short cuts. You can, for instance, grow a self-blanching variety. This matures quickly and is ready for use in the late summer. It does not have the crisp, nutty flavour of the winter varieties, but it is good all the same and helps to vary salads and other dishes. It cooks well and there is hardly any waste.

If you do not object to its appearance, the American Green or Tendercrisp is another summer variety. Both of these should be grown the same way, that is, not in long rows but in blocks, the plants 9in apart. The blanching process can be speeded up by placing boards or black plastic sheeting around the block of self-blanching celery. Alternatively, the plants can be grown in frames.

The way of raising and subsequently hardening and planting any of the celery plants is the same as for celeriac. Celery plants are often on sale in garden centres, but it is generally wise to order them early in the season.

There are three varieties of the crisper winter kinds of celery: red, pink and white. The red appears to be the hardiest and is usually still good in the new year. White seems to be the most popular but if you have only ever tasted this kind, I suggest you try some pink to compare flavours.

The most important factor for success is to ensure that the plants never become dry at the roots. Celery in the wild is a marshland plant and in spite of the considerable difference between the cultivated varieties and the wild species, their demand for adequate water during growth remains the same. For this reason traditional culture calls for trenches to be dug, some 8–12in deep. This makes it possible to flood the earth from time to time and to keep the water around the plants for a longer period of time.

I am always ready to challenge traditional methods, and today's garden watering appliances are so good that it is possible to grow splendid crops by using one of these instead of trenching. Compromise by spacing young celery plants in deep drills such as you might make for pea seeds, and install a trickle irrigation unit along the row. As well as watering, liquid feeding is important. Apply this at times after the plants have been well watered, while the soil is receptive. Superphosphate is a good celery fertiliser. Give the plants an application about 4 weeks after they are planted and another a month or so later. Use 1oz to 6ft of row, very little really, and don't overdo it.

In August or September, by which time the plants should be well grown and at least 10in tall, one has to think about blanching their stems. The dark green stems of the winter varieties may have a bitter flavour. For this reason plants are earthed up. First of all the stems are tied together with raffia so that they are neatly cupped and then soil from each side of them is drawn up the stems as high as the leaves. To save this labour, various other means are often employed. Paper collars, drain pipes and black plastic tubes or bags can be used instead. The moist soil attracts slugs and they seem to esteem celery, so where they are a pest put down slug bait or pellets.

Before earthing up the plants just do a little grooming. Side shoots or low-growing leaves are best removed so that only stem area is covered. These odds and ends will be useful in the kitchen.

If you want to try your hand at the traditional method, remember that the trenches must be precisely dug. They should have firm, upright sides well batted into shape, otherwise they may cave in and submerge the young plants.

As you can imagine, considerable space is taken this way and personally I find it irritating to see so much empty land for such a long period. It is customary to grow a catch crop on top of the ridge on each side of the trench. Radish, lettuce and summer spinach are crops used for this purpose.

Once the trench is made it should be floored with a good deep layer of well-rotted animal manure. This should then be forked into the base of the trench so that the soil is rich and well aerated. It is best to prepare the trench some weeks before planting so that the soil can settle.

Set the plants outdoors in June or July in the base of the trench 10–12in apart in a single row or 12in apart each way in a double row. The width of the trench will depend on this.

After planting, the trench should receive its first flooding. Let the water run in until it settles in the base of the trench. Continue this process during dry spells.

Cooking
After I have cleaned and prepared a head of celery I reckon to have only the merest amount to throw away. I mention this having once watched one of my home helps clean a head and prepare to consign more than half its weight to the dustbin. All the healthy leaves can be used as flavouring. Those which have become blanched can be incorporated into a mixed salad. Dark green pieces of stem also can be used to flavour stock or bouillon. These will keep for several days. The pale green tips of blanched stalks, even the thinner leaf stalks, can be cut into sections and stewed and served as a vegetable. These are very good served in a bechamel-type sauce made from stock and with a little cream added at the last minute. You can use fish stock if you are serving the celery with fish. In this case the stems are improved in flavour and appearance if they are garnished with some of the blanched leaves finely chopped. Chervil also suits the flavour of celery.

These stem pieces can be mixed with other vegetables to make an attractive mixture. They look good with carrot slices and tiny white onions. Garnish them with parsley or chervil.

For salads, slice the stems finely and mix with many good things to make crisp winter salads. They go well with apples, carrots, leeks, all raw and finely sliced also; cream cheese, walnuts, and if you like a touch of sweet-tasting food in a salad, with dates and dried fruits. Celery slices can be mixed into yogurt with 1tbsp mixed herbs, and used as a dressing. Chop them finer still and add them to a creamy soup ust before serving.

You can use them with a good proportion of the shredded blanched leaves as a base for a prawn or some other fish cocktail. Half fill the glasses with the celery mixture, arrange the fish on this and pour the dressing over it (see Herbs).

The crisp blanched stems can also be used this way. If you find that the outer ones are a little fibrous it is a simple matter to string them. Cut a slice from the base and pull this towards the tip. Usually each time you slice the stem another fibre is released and this can simply be pulled away.

Stems that are cupped can be cut into conveniently sized sections and filled in various ways to serve as cocktail or party snacks or as hors d'oeuvres. Use cream cheese with a little chives, or some spicy seed such as caraway or cumin is a popular filling. Using cream cheese as a base you can adapt it as you will, adding chopped olives or tinned fish. Shrimps are especially good. Instead of cream cheese you can use scrambled egg into which a few shreds of smoked salmon, kipper, or 1tsp mock caviar have been blended.

The thick root portion of celery can be cleaned, pared and then grated and used in a salad or to flavour a sauce. If the celery is soaked for a few hours in clean, slightly salted water it becomes really crisp, but if you wish to keep it for several days it is best not to wash it. I like always to have some really fresh celery on Boxing Day and other days following Christmas. I lift the heads from the ground well in advance of this date, usually as the weather allows and dry them by leaving them on newspaper in the air for a while. I then wrap them in more newspaper and keep them in an insulated picnic box which is kept on a stone floor in an outer pantry. Stored in a cold, dark, dry place, the celery will keep for a week or more. Prepare it some hours in advance so that it will become really crisp and cold. Celery which has been washed can be stored in covered plastic containers and kept in the refrigerator for several days, but it may become a little discoloured.

Baked Hearts of Celery

If you have raised such a good crop of celery that you can spare some hearts for cooking, try them this way:

1 celery heart per person	1 medium carrot, 1 medium
2 rashers streaky bacon	onion, both finely sliced
bay leaf, sprig parsley, lovage	good white stock—I suggest that
if you have it	you use a pig's trotter or
	knuckle for this

Wash and then blanch the hearts in boiling salted water for 10min. Line a casserole with the bacon. Strew the onion and carrot on the base of the casserole and lay the hearts on them. Add the stock and seasoning. Preheat the oven to a moderate temperature. Bring the casserole slowly to the boil on the stove and then transfer it to the oven. Cook for 1–1½hr. If you wish to make this a more substantial dish you can cover it with grated cheese and brown this before serving.

Baked Celery Custards (serves 6)

This dish can be made in one vessel, but these individual custards are good starters for a meal. Serve hot or cold.

6tbsp finely sliced celery sections	grated Parmesan cheese
2 eggs	salt, pepper, bay leaf
¾pt milk	1tbsp parsley or chervil
nut of butter	nutmeg

First blanch the celery for 10min in the butter. Drain it and put it with the milk, seasoning and bay leaf in a saucepan and let all simmer until the celery is quite tender. Strain and measure out the celery into the dishes. Beat the eggs and mix them with the milk. Pour this over the celery in equal quantities. Sprinkle the herb and a little cheese over the top of the custard in each dish and then sprinkle the tops liberally with nutmeg. Stand the dishes in a baking tin with water halfway up their sides. Bake at 275° F, 135° C for 1hr.

MORELLO CHERRIES

Growing
A fan-trained tree is the most convenient. It is doubly useful because it grows splendidly on a north or north-west wall. Cherries can be bought ready trained. They also make neat bushes.

This type of cherry is self-fertile, which means that you do not have to plant other varieties of cherries near it. It will cross with other cherries though, if these happen to be in the vicinity. It is one of the few sour cherries and is not fit for eating raw. Its fruits can be harvested in August and September.

Sour cherries can be grown on a greater range of soils than the sweet varieties, but they must be given good drainage as well as adequate protection from cold winds and spring frosts.

When they are grown as bushes, these cherries should be trained as little as possible. When fan-trained they should be encouraged to make new shoots. It is usual to tie the branches which make up the fan to a series of parallel wires, or alternatively a plastic covered mesh can be used.

The fruits are always formed on new shoots that were grown in the previous season. To promote these the terminal shoots should be pinched out when they are about 3–4in long. This will induce the stem to produce laterals. Surplus shoots should be pinched out when they are quite small. Those that are left should be tied to the training wires or trellis. From this you can tell that it is best to retain those which are most easily and conveniently tied. They should not cross each other. Usually just two or three laterals are kept.

To keep cherries in good health and full production and also to restore old bushes which you might have inherited if you have an old garden, give them a mulch of well-decayed farmyard manure in spring. If this is not obtainable apply nitro-chalk, 2–3oz per sq yd. In autumn also apply sulphate of potash, 1–2oz per sq yd.

If you grow your tree against a wall, water it well in dry spells and feed it occasionally with liquid manure.

Cooking

These fruits are easily and variously preserved. Perhaps less well known are the ways they can be pickled, when they are delicious with many kinds of cold meats. For instance, remove the stalks and place the cherries in an oven dish, cover with brown sugar and bake very slowly until the fruit is soft. When cool put them in a glass jar and cover with aromatic vinegar, flavoured if you wish with thyme, tarragon and bay. These cherries should be kept at least a fortnight before being used.

Prepare the vinegar by heating 1qt vinegar with 1 cup of brown sugar, 1–2in stick cinnamon, 3 cloves and a saltspoon of nutmeg.

Sour cherries are best cooked lightly covered with sugar in a covered dish and slowly baked in an oven. When they are soft proceed with various recipes. They are delicious served with meringue, where the sweet of one complements the sharpness of the other.

You can also make a delicious 'flan' by using creamed rice as a base. Make a layer of the rice about 1in deep in a heatproof dish. Pile the cooked cherries on this covering the rice almost to its edges. Cover them with ordinary meringue mixture. Heap it up attractively. Sprinkle a little icing sugar on this. Place it in a moderate oven to set. Serve hot or cold. In my opinion it is nicest cold.

Whipped Cherries

1qt stoned cherries	1oz powdered gelatine
1 cup sugar	3 egg whites
⅓ cup water	pinch salt

Boil the sugar and ⅓ cup of water until a syrup is made—about 10min fast boiling. Add the cherries and simmer for 3–5min. Drain the fruit. Mix the gelatine with 2tbsp cold water and then pour the cherry juice over it. It should measure 1 cup (½pt). Cool, and place the liquid in the refrigerator for it to set. Later, whip this with an egg beater or a blender until it is fluffy. Beat the egg whites with the salt until they are quite stiff. Fold them into the whipped juice. Have ready a jelly mould or a soufflé dish made wet inside. Pour in a little at a time, making sandwiches of the whip and the cherries. Chill the mould until it is set. To serve, turn it out and decorate with a few cherries and angelica 'leaves'. This recipe can be adapted to most fruits.

Morello Cherry Jam

Measure the cherries and an equal quantity of sugar. Place the stoned cherries in a dish, sprinkle a little of the sugar over them and heat in a covered dish in a warm oven until the fruit is soft. Heat the sugar in a dish in the oven. Transfer the cherries to a preserving pan, add the sugar and boil together until the jam sets when tested. Pour into hot jars and cover.

Glacé Cherries

Prepare a good heavy syrup of sugar and water. Let it boil and put the stoned cherries into the syrup. Simmer until soft. Leave them standing in the syrup for 3 days. Drain and place them in a bowl. Bring the syrup to the boil again and pour it over the cherries and then leave them for another 3 days. Drain and dry them on a sieve. Store in greaseproof paper in jars.

You can use the syrup to sweeten fruit salads or to make crème caramels.

CHERVIL

Growing
You'll never regret growing this little herb, which is as useful as parsley. It is not unlike it in appearance but its flavour is more delicate and slightly reminiscent of aniseed.

It is ready to use 6–8 weeks after sowing and is best sown in short rows in succession, beginning in March. It will seed itself if you give it a little corner somewhere. You can also sow it in boxes to grow indoors for winter supply. Thin out, but do not try to transplant. It will grow almost anywhere.

I can gather chervil even in winter, for it has colonised itself in part of my garden. But you may want to dry it, in which case simply gather, wash, pat dry and spread it out to dry thoroughly, away from strong sunlight.

Cooking
In sauces for fish dishes. Chop it for soups and all kinds of salads.

CHICORY

Growing
You might not get such good-looking chicons as those which are imported from specialist growers, but you will get edible hearts at a time when salad prices are high.

Sow the seed in shallow drills $\frac{1}{2}$in deep in May or June. Be sure that the soil is good and rich, because the plants must grow strong, vital roots. It is these which you have to lift and force.

As soon as the plants are large enough to handle, thin them out to 9in apart.

Leave them to grow until November, when you should lift them and get them ready for forcing. It is best to lift the roots as you need them if you are in a mild area, otherwise lift them all at one time and store them outdoors in some sheltered place, stood upright in sand or ashes.

To grow the chicons use deep flower pots, boxes, or some other deep containers. As a guide you should plant 3 or 4 roots to a 7in pot.

If you have grown them well the tap roots should be long, a little parsnip-like in appearance and unbranched. Cut off the leafy tops to within 1in of the crown. If necessary trim back the roots from the base so that they fit into the container. They should stand upright.

Use ordinary soil to almost fill the pots. If you can top this with a really deep layer of clean horticultural sand, so much the better. Water the soil after planting and allow it to drain.

To force, bring the pots into a temperature of 60° F, 16° C. They will grow in the kitchen if you have no other place. In a greenhouse they can go under the staging. The chicons must be forced in complete darkness. If you use flower pots, stand an equally sized pot upside down over the planted one and plug its drainage hole to exclude all light. Alternatively pull a black plastic bag over the tops. Leave room for the leaves to grow. You should see these in about 3 weeks.

But here is a simpler method than the foregoing and one which you can also use to force rhubarb, seakale and dandelions. You need a strong black plastic bag. Its size doesn't matter so long as you can find room for it when it is filled. Place a 3in layer of moist peat in the base. Press this down so that the bag stands firmly. Tuck in the corners first. Plant the roots you intend to force, packing and wedging them into place with more peat and take this up as far as their crowns. Close the bag, making sure that it does not collapse and sink down to rest on top of the crowns. If you have sufficient breath, blow! Stand it in a warm place. Inspect it after 2 or 3 weeks for rate of growth.

Cooking

Chicory is delicious in salad. There is little waste, for usually only one or two faded outer leaves need removing. Wash and dry the head, peel off and pat dry the leaves as you separate them. They are usually served whole, but you can also cut them across. They are best with French dressing. Alternatively use a mayonnaise, cream or yogurt dressing.

Chicory goes well with walnuts and the two together with a cream cheese and plenty of fresh green herbs make a delicious salad. Orange also blends well and I sometimes make a dressing with orange juice and oil instead of either lemon juice or vinegar.

Epicures praise cooked chicory. It has a slightly bitter flavour and if you like cooked lettuce you will like this.

Braised Chicory with Bacon (serves 4)

4 gammon rashers	2 medium onions finely chopped
4 heads chicory	1tbsp flour
1oz butter	2 good sprigs parsley
1 large carrot finely sliced	1 cup good stock

Melt the butter in a lidded oven dish. Wrap each rasher around a chicory head. Gently fry the onion and carrot until soft but not browned. Lay the chicory-bacon rolls on these. Turn them once so that all surface is firmed, put in the parsley, cover the dish and simmer for 10min. Pour in the stock, recover the pan and bake slowly at 375° F, 190° C for 30min. Take from oven and thicken the sauce with the flour, first mixed to a paste with a little cold stock.

Garnish with chopped parsley and serve with mashed potatoes or pasta.

CHIVES

Growing

Chives are best lifted and divided frequently. Spring is the best time for this. The plants grow surprisingly well and quickly, going on providing 'grass' until late autumn, so long, that is, as the foliage is cut frequently and they are growing in good soil with plenty of sunshine. They will grow anywhere except on cold and heavy clay. I grow a row of chives along a path and I lift and divide alternate plants each spring, pulling the plants apart and replanting smaller portions.

If you do this you are almost sure to have too many chives, but if you care to pot a few at the same time you will have some plants which you can set aside to bring indoors and force in winter. They will grow well on a sunny window-sill. You can raise chives from seed indoors sown in late winter and spring.

Cooking

Essential to good cooks, chives impart a faint but distinctive onion flavour to soups, sauces, omelettes and many other dishes. Furthermore, the bright green of the finely sliced 'grass' is both attractive and appetising.

Cut the chives close to the soil. Tie the bunch so that you can wash the leaves easily. Pat dry and cut across either with a very sharp knife or with scissors, beginning at the base. Stand the bunch in water if you do not use it all at once. It will keep fresh for a few days.

If you have several plants you can work your way through them and by the time you have started on the last the first should have grown and be ready for use again.

Do not put chives in a dish until just before you serve it—they will then stay bright green.

CORN SALAD

Growing

One of the most useful and simply grown winter salads is corn salad, *Valerianella locusta*, sometimes called lamb's lettuce. It is considered especially suitable for pheasant and any other similar game and at one time was always to be found on the rich man's table. Try it with cold meats of any kind.

Sow it in shallow drills, in a dry sunny place, fortnightly from August to September. Thin the seedlings to about 6in apart when they have grown to the three-leaf stage. I keep my corn salad under cloches. It is more succulent then, but this is not essential for it is quite hardy.

Corn salad matures in 6–8 weeks. You can gather the leaves separately as you do for spinach, or by cutting the entire plant as you do for lettuce.

Cooking

I like this salad with a French dressing. You will find it useful to mix with other greens and this is a good way to spin out a head of chicory and a little lettuce.

You can cook it in exactly the same way as you cook spinach. Often in spring when the plants begin to grow apace and when other greens are either scarce or unvaried, this is a good way to deal with and clear this crop.

If you have a freezer
Treat as spinach.

COURGETTES OR ZUCCINI

Growing
These are a variety of gourd or marrow. The plants are neat and compact. Sow the seeds as directed for marrows and plant out or space 3ft apart each way.

You can let courgettes grow to their full size, which is quite considerable, but in some ways this is a waste as they are then not so prolific. The best way is to gather them as soon as the flower on the end of them fades. They will then be about the size of a sausage. This is really the best guide for gathering, because the length of the fruits varies among varieties.

There is now a golden courgette.

Cooking
Courgettes need no peeling. You can cook them in any way recommended for marrow. Since they are so small they can be cooked whole.

To boil them, simply put them in a pan with enough water to cover the bottom and a little olive oil, butter or margarine and salt. Bring to the boil and simmer for 6–8min.

Or chop a clove of garlic and heat this in a pan with enough olive oil to cover the bottom of the pan. Wash and wipe the courgettes and slice them thinly. Gently fry them until they are tender. Take out, season with salt and paprika and scatter chopped marjoram or basil over them and serve.

Courgettes in Batter

Dip the raw slices in light batter (see Cauliflowers Fried) and fry in deep fat. Drain well and serve while they are still crisp.

Courgettes for Salad

Halve the courgettes. Do not peel. Boil and drain. Lay them on a piece of kitchen paper for a few moments and then place them on a dish and pour French dressing on them while they are still warm. Sprinkle with a mixture of chopped chives, chervil and tarragon.

Courgettes can also be used raw in salads. The new golden variety looks good served this way. Leave them unskinned if they are as young and tender as they should be.

Courgettes and Rice

Cut courgettes in half. Roll in rashers of streaky bacon and grill. Boil rice. Arrange the grilled rolls on a bed of rice. Garnish with chopped chives. Serve with the melted bacon fat.

Courgette Flowers

Courgette flowers are delicious to eat. The first time I tried them was in Florence where they had been fried in batter and were served cold as an hors d'oeuvre. Cooked vegetables are often served cold in Italy. But these fritters are delicious hot.

Sometimes the flowers are stuffed with rice (a good way of using a

73

left-over pilaff) or minced meats, then dipped in batter and fried.
Make the batter as follows:

2 heaped tbsp self-raising flour	**3tbsp water**
1 egg	**pepper, salt**
1tbsp olive oil	

Put the flour into a basin, make a well in the centre with the back of
a spoon or fork. Break in the egg, add the oil and the seasoning. Beat
these together using a fork, gradually bringing in the flour from the
sides of the basin. Add the water. Go on mixing until this is well
blended. Dip the flowers. Fry in deep fat until golden.

If you have a freezer
Courgettes are among the most highly appreciated of vegetables from
my freezer, especially in mid-winter.

When plants are properly productive they can be gathered every
day. Blanch tiny ones whole for 2min. Larger ones can be split down
the centre.

CRESS

Growing
First, the kind of cress which goes with mustard. It is best to grow this
in succession, filling a series of boxes, trays or pans, starting with three
or four and re-sowing them as they are used.

Partially fill the containers with sifted soil. Firm the surface and sow
the seed so that it makes an even mat and covers the soil. Press the seeds
gently into the soil surface, water the box, cover it with a sheet of
polythene, a sheet of glass or even a sheet of paper and stand it on a
window-sill, in a greenhouse or frame. Uncover as soon as germination
takes place.

Cut the cress with scissors as soon as the seed leaves have fully ex-
panded. Grow mustard in the same way as for cress but sow the seed
3 days later because it germinates more quickly.

Cooking
Make cress eggs. Hard boil the eggs, shell and cut in half lengthwise.

Remove the yolks. Using ¼oz butter to every egg, pound the yolks and butter until blended. Chop the cress and mix 1 level tbsp cress to each egg. When blended, fill the white halves. Serve with sliced tomato salad.

Growing land cress

Land cress is similar in taste and appearance to water cress. It will be both large leaved and truly succulent if given a good rich but ordinary soil. It really is well worth growing and very easy. You need a moist, partially shaded border. This is a good plant to grow as an edging along a path where it will be easy to pick.

Sow from March until June for summer salads, in September for winter. If covered with cloches during this time the plants produce extra tender leaves.

Do not let the plants become dry in hot weather.

Land cress is really a perennial, but it is best to lift old plants and sow annually. Do not let them flower and seed or you will have land cress everywhere!

Cooking land cress

Use this crop in every way that you would use watercress, as a garnish, or in salads, soups and sandwiches.

Try this as a salad dressing, it's delicious and very nutritious. Sieve or blend 2 hard-boiled eggs. Mix them into a paste with just enough olive oil to make them fluid. Stir in ¼pt French dressing and a good dash of lemon juice. Mix into this ½ cup of chopped land cress. This transforms cold meat.

Cress makes a fine and distinctive soup.

Potage Purée de Cresson Alenois (Creamed Cress)

½lb cress   ½lb potatoes sliced thinly
3tbsp butter melted in heavy pan   milk, cream
1qt good stock

Wash and chop the cress and add it to the melted butter. Add the stock and potatoes. Simmer until tender. Sieve or blend. Thin with milk and stock to the required consistency. Serve after adding a little butter and cream. This makes a really substantial first course so follow it with a light dish.

Growing watercress

Watercress is easily grown if there is a sunny but damp spot in your garden. You don't need a spring but you will have to provide plenty of water from time to time.

Make a bed by removing some of the soil. Line the bed with at least 6in of well-rotted animal manure or home-made garden compost. Cover this with 3in of soil and a good sprinkling of peat and on this sow the seeds. Or you can save some rooted cuttings from a bought bunch and plant these. Flood the bed to begin with and again from time to time when the weather is dry.

Sow thinly and be sure to keep the baby seedlings moist. Transplant or thin them to about 6in apart each way. Remember that the more you water these plants the better they will grow. Divide them in May or August.

CUCUMBERS

Growing

Outdoor growing is such a simple way of growing cucumbers. 'Indoors' means in a greenhouse, or in a frame, usually classified as 'under glass'. The varieties for this method of culture are distinct from those which can be grown with no glass protection at all. Usually the seedsman lists the one as 'House or Frame Varieties' and the outdoor kinds as 'Ridge'. At one time these plants, like marrows, were always grown on ridges, but this practice is dying out. The purpose of the ridge was to support the trailing stems and to make the fruits easier to gather. Often the soil in the ridges was of a special mixture.

Modern varieties of outdoor cucumbers are very good indeed. Careful breeding has resulted in a race of fruits which contain no bitterness do not cause indigestion, are resistant to disease and extremely easy to grow. These modern varieties, such as the Burpless, Japanese Kyoto and Kaga and Ochai Long Day, produce an abundance of fruit for a minimum of effort.

Sow the seeds singly in small pots indoors in mid-April, in a greenhouse, a warm frame or on an indoor window-sill. Harden the plants off in May by standing them outdoors on all possible occasions, bringing them indoors at nights. Plant outdoors the first week in June.

Give them rich soil. Prepare each site by taking out a square 18in wide and 12in deep and filling it with a mixture of 2 parts soil, 1 part well-rotted manure or home-made compost and 1 part peat.

If you prefer, you can sow the seed directly in these sites in May instead of raising the plants indoors. Cover them with cloches if you can.

When the plants are in flower give them a dressing of some complete plant fertiliser.

There are many good, quick-maturing and delicious varieties nowadays. If you want to pickle your own gherkins you need to grow a special variety, Dobie's Prolific for example.

Keep gathering the fruits and more will form.

Cooking (see also Dill)
Ideal for salads, sandwiches and hors d'oeuvres. Try them cut into 2in chunks, centres scooped out and the pulp mixed with cream cheese and chives and refilled. Use the cucumbers as a delicately flavoured base in dishes like this one.

Cucumber Jelly Starters

2tbsp gelatine
2tbsp cold water
1½ cups (¾pt) white stock
1 clove garlic, 1 small shallot, both chopped finely
sprig parsley
stalk of celery with leaves when in season, alternatively use Florence fennel
½tsp salt
2 large cucumbers

Soak the gelatine in the water. Boil the stock with the herbs and add the gelatine and salt to it. Strain. Peel and grate the cucumbers and stir them into the liquid. Strain. Colour it green if you wish. When it thickens slightly stir it again. Divide the jelly into small dishes. When firm you can decorate each in various ways, with mixed chopped herbs nuts, cream cheese, seeded tomatoes or what you will.

Eastern Cucumber Salad (serves 6)

The new Burpless cucumbers are excellent for this dish. Prepare the cucumbers by cutting them in half lengthwise and then peeling them very thinly. You can use a potato peeler for this. Cutting the cucumbers first facilitates slicing them this way.

2 cups of cucumber slices	1tbsp vinegar or lemon juice
$\frac{1}{2}$tsp salt	1 cup yogurt
1 clove garlic finely chopped and then pounded (do this in a bowl in which you are to mix the salad, then you will not waste any)	1tbsp finely chopped mint
	some small borage leaves and flowers

Blend the yogurt, garlic, salt, vinegar and chopped mint in the serving bowl. Add the cucumber. Mix these well so that all are coated with the dressing. Chill. Decorate with the leaves and flowers before serving.

Pickled gherkins

Gather the little cucumbers very young, as soon as the flower has faded from the end. If you haven't enough at one time to fill a jar, keep them in the refrigerator in a plastic box or bag, for they must not dry out.

You will need: vinegar—preferably a white wine vinegar which is not so coarse—sprigs of dill, thyme, bay leaf, cloves, small white pickling onions or tiny shallots (optional).

First rub the little fruits all over with a clean cloth to remove the down. Place them in a bowl and cover them with coarse salt, preferably sea salt. Leave them for 24hr. Drain and wash them in a bowl containing water with a dash of vinegar. Drain and wipe them dry.

Arrange the gherkins in a jar with a sprig of each herb, the bay leaf, two cloves and a few onions to each 2lb jar. Cover with vinegar. Seal the jars. The gherkins will be ready to eat after about 5 weeks.

CURRANTS

Growing blackcurrants

These luscious fruits ripen later than the red and white currants—from July to early September according to the variety.

Soil for them must be rich, well dug and properly prepared. It is almost impossible to make the soil too rich for them. In addition to preparation the soil must be kept fed, in the spring with 2oz sulphate of ammonia per sq yd and again in the autumn with sulphate of potash, 1oz per sq yd. Deep mulches of animal manure, home-made compost and grass cuttings will help keep the roots moist (essential), discourage weeds and help to rejuvenate the soil.

Blackcurrants should be pruned as soon as the fruit is gathered. One of the best ways to do this is to carry out both operations at the same time. Cut the fruiting branches to just below the lowest bunch of currants and carry them to a bench or table where the fruit can be picked from them in comparative comfort. Any shoots which have not fruited can be slightly shortened. Really old growths can be cut close to the ground in winter, but summer pruning is best. Fruits are formed on the previous season's shoots.

One advantage that these currants have over the other two is that they will tolerate a certain amount of shade, and for this reason one sometimes sees them planted among larger fruit trees.

The bushes are not too utilitarian in appearance except perhaps when netted, so they can be grown near a flower border should this be the only space available.

Growing red and white currants

These are plants to play with, for they can be trained as cordons with one, two or three stems, or as fans against walls and fences or on wires. Like the Morello cherry these fruits will grow well on a north-facing wall or fence. Indeed, you can spin out the crop this way by growing early fruits in a sunny place and later ones on the north side. Trained fruits are easier to net, but these can also be grown as standards. You will have to wait a year or two longer for your fruit if you want to train your bushes, but standards do mean that you can grow one crop well above another, a form of two-tier gardening.

Red and white currents are easy to grow and seem to be more

tolerant of poorer soils than blackcurrants. They stand drought better and they do not need as much nitrogen in the soil. They can be given an annual boost with 1oz per sq yd of sulphate of ammonia in the spring and the same quantity of sulphate of potash in the winter.

It is as well to remember that these plants, like their decorative cousins of the shrub border, bloom early and so should not be planted where frosts are likely to harm them.

Bushes should be planted 5ft each way for all kinds. Single cordons can be planted 1ft apart, double 1½ft, and triple cordons 2ft.

Red and white currants are pruned differently from blackcurrants. The fruit is produced on the old wood. They should be pruned hard in the winter and again, not so severely, in summer. In the first case shorten the main or leading shoots by a third and cut the side shoots back to two or three buds. In July, shorten the side shoots so that they carry only 5 leaves. Leave the main shoots until winter.

Cooking

Currants are most easily stripped from the bunch if you use a fork. Hold a bunch over a basin with one hand and draw the fork down the stem with the other hand. The currants will fall easily into the basin and you will prevent your fingers from becoming stained. You should use a silver fork.

Green currants—unripe red and white varieties—are delicious when cooked. So if you are short of fruit there is really no need to wait until all of these are coloured. Take the opportunity of thinning out some of the thickest clusters or the most heavily laden branches.

Surprisingly, these green currants do not need quite so much sugar as the riper fruits.

Redcurrant Jelly

Perhaps this is the most popular of all dishes made from this fruit. It is not necessary to stem or strip the currants.

Measure the fruit and allow a quarter of their bulk of water in which to stew them. Too much water will mean that the jelly will take a long time to solidify. You can even make this jelly with no water at all if you wish.

Crush the currants in the preserving pan from time to time as they cook and soften. When they have lost their colour the juice will be expelled from them. Drain all through a jelly bag and let this drip for some hours. Measure the juice. Allow an equal measure of sugar. Heat the sugar in the oven and when hot add to the juices in the pan. Boil rapidly for 5min and then begin to test. When the liquid solidifies pour it into warmed jars. Cover.

Crystallised Red and White Currants

Select the best bunches of currants you can find. Wash them and let them drain on kitchen paper. They must be quite dry. Take 1 gill of water and 2 egg whites. (Halve this if you intend to do only a few fruits.) Beat the eggs to a peak and then add the water and mix it well. Have ready a small dish with a little fine sugar in it and some more to use later, and some lightly sugared paper on which to lay the fruit to dry. Hold the currants by the stem and dip them in the egg white so that they are really well coated. Let any surplus drain off and then roll the bunch in the sugar. I find it best to use a little sugar at a time otherwise the bulk of it gets wet. When the bunch is well coated, lay it down on the sugared paper. Allow several hours for the fruit to dry properly. Let it remain in a dry place.

Rödgröd med Flöde

This is a delicious Danish dish, a sweet which is sometimes served as supper. Children like it and it is both full of flavour and vitamins.

1lb redcurrants	2oz blackcurrants
½lb raspberries	2oz sago

Stew the fruit in enough water to cover the bottom of the pan. When the fruit is soft strain it through a sieve. Bring it back to the boil, but reserve enough to mix with the sago to make a smooth liaison. Add this to the boiling juice and stir well for 2min. Remove the pan from the heat and continue to stir the mixture until it is cool. Pour it into individual glasses and serve with cream and sugar.

DAMSONS

Growing

It seems to me that more people inherit old damson trees than set about planting new ones. Yet these are good, productive trees to have in a garden and one has the joy of the blossom as well. An important factor in their favour is that they can be used to make an excellent windbreak. For this purpose pyramidal trees should be planted close together. A good fruit nurseryman will advise on what varieties are most likely to suit your particular needs. For isolated trees most damsons today are usually grown as half-standards, but I must admit a weakness for the full standard. Its shape and habit appeal to me.

Damsons should receive roughly the same treatment for cultivation as plums.

They ripen later than plums, usually in September and October. Although the fruits resemble each other, damsons cannot really be eaten raw in the same way as a luscious dessert plum. A true damson should be much smaller than a plum, almost black, with a yellow-green flesh which has an astringent quality. Often bullaces, a fruit which ripens even later, are sold as damsons in the shops.

Cooking

A damson pie has an aroma and flavour you will not find in any other fruit. Damsons bottle well, make good jams, cheeses, wines and pickles.

Damson Wine

8lb damsons	2lb sugar to each gal of juice
1gal water	

Bruise the fruit by bashing it with a pestle or wooden spoon, not metal. Put it in a large bowl. Pour the boiling water on it. Let it stand for 48hr and then strain into a bucket or bowl. Measure and add sugar accordingly. Stir well until the sugar dissolves. Cover. Skim if necessary from time to time. Bottle when fermentation ceases. Damsons have their own yeast but you can add yeast if you prefer to do so.

DANDELIONS

Growing

I don't plant these but I do let them grow in certain places about the garden. In the early spring when I see a good plant either in the vegetable garden or in one of the borders I cover it with an earthenware flower pot, close the hole with a cork and slip a few slug pellets near the rim. In a week or two the leaves will have become blanched and they can be cut and served as a salad or even cooked.

If you do grow lots of dandelions, please remember that they should not be allowed to go to seed. Your neighbours may not be as fond of them as you are. You can buy seeds of dandelion, *Taraxacum officinale*, and these cultivated forms usually have thicker leaves than the wild species. Sow them in 1in deep drills in April. Thin the plants to 6in apart in May. Keep the flower stems picked off.

Instead of waiting as I do until the spring to force those which are growing in the garden, you can lift the roots in November and store them in sand in a cool place as you do chicory. Grow the roots in exactly the same way.

Cooking

Blanched dandelion leaves mix well with other green salad materials, particularly corn salad and land cress. Try this method of serving which can also be used for lettuce and chicory.

Bacon Dressing Salad (serves 4)

1 rasher of fat bacon	2tbsp vinegar
1tbsp sugar	1pt washed leaves (it is difficult
1tsp French mustard	to give a measure)
$\frac{1}{2}$tsp salt	1 small onion
pepper	1 small shallot

Cut bacon into small pieces and brown in frying pan. When it is crisp remove it and add the sugar, salt, pepper and mustard to the hot fat. Mix well, add the vinegar, remove from heat and allow to cool a little. Have the leaves and finely sliced onion and shallot mixed ready. Pour the warm dressing over these and add the bacon. Mix well and serve.

To keep dandelion leaves white when they are washed, bruise them as little as possible and put a slice of lemon in the basin or bowl of water. Leave the leaves to soak for an hour or so. For salads, drain and dry on kitchen paper.

Young tender green leaves can be cooked as spinach.

They also make an excellent spring soup. Cook them first in a little olive oil and just the water which adheres to the leaves after washing them. When they are cooked, blend or sieve them. Make a bechamel sauce as a base for the soup, using 1oz butter, 1oz flour and ½pt milk to each cup of purée.

I like to begin my sauce by 'melting' a clove of garlic and a shallot, both finely chopped, in the butter. Add flour and quickly blend with the butter. Stir in the milk, hot or cold to a smooth paste. Add the dandelions. Just before serving remove from the heat and stir in a well-beaten egg. This is optional, but it does give a lovely silky quality to the soup. If you want to serve the soup as a meal rather than a single course, serve it with grated cheese and croutons. Crisp bacon pieces also make a good garnish.

DILL

Growing

Dill is an attractive, feathery annual, an umbellifer which grows from 18in to almost 3ft according to its situation. The seed should be sown in April, or early May if the season is late or cold, where the plants are to flower and in a sunny, open site. Sow the seed thinly and thin out the seedlings as soon as this is practicable to give the plants 6in each way.

At this time also provide supports. Twiggy sticks are best, but not always easily or cheaply available. Failing these use thin bamboos and strong thread or garden twine as you might for peas. The plants are best grown in a block rather than a row. Once tall they are apt to keel over unless supported. Keep them clean and soil-free.

If the soil is moist it is possible to transplant young seedlings.

Cooking

The distinctive flavour of this herb is greatly esteemed by Russian, Scandinavian and other north European cooks. They make a simple dill sauce by browning a little flour in melted butter, adding stock and stirring until it thickens, and then adding 1tbsp chopped dill.

In many other countries the flowers and seed heads are used in pickles and to make dill vinegar, which incidentally is delicious with fish. Dill usually accompanies fish, egg and cheese dishes and in foreign recipes is mainly used with cabbage and potatoes. Seed is sprinkled over these and young leaves are boiled with potatoes in the same way as mint. Very young leaves or young flower heads are the best. The old leaves have too strong and coarse a flavour. Dill loses its flavour when dried.

As you will know if you like dill pickles, this herb goes well with the cool flavour of cucumber. Try it, or the seeds, in cucumber sandwiches.

Dill Pickles

I find dill pickles so useful to give a little variety to dishes—for instance, chopped and added to a white sauce for fish, chopped with fresh green herbs in yogurt as a salad dressing, sliced thinly in sandwiches with meat or cheese or chopped and mixed with grated cheese, nuts and cream as a salad.

Gherkins will do, but the fat cucumbers are best. Gather them when they are about 3in long. The following quantities will fill four 2lb preserving jars. It is a little difficult to give exact quantities, but if you haven't enough cucumbers you can always save some of the pickle vinegar until you have more.

2qt vinegar
1qt water
1 cup ($\frac{1}{2}$pt) coarse salt
4 cloves garlic
24 peppercorns

4 cloves
4 bay leaves
4 flower heads dill
4 blackcurrant leaves (optional)

Thoroughly clean and completely dry the cucumbers. Put the spices and garlic at the bottom of the jars. Pack the cucumbers in, vertically is usually the best way. Cover with a blackcurrant leaf. Boil the vinegar, water and salt together. Stand the jars on a board to prevent them cracking and pour in the boiling liquid. Cover lightly until they have cooled. Seal. You can begin eating them after 5 days.

ENDIVES

Growing

This crop will give you fine salads for autumn and winter.

Sow in shallow drills in April for late summer and autumn, June or July for late autumn and winter crops. As soon as the seedlings are large enough to handle transplant into good, rich soil, 1ft apart each way.

Endives are dark green in colour and should be blanched because the leaves are indigestible. Blanching in the garden differs from blanching in cookery. To blanch, wait until the plants are almost full grown. Bring the outer leaves up from the ground until they are upright and tie them securely in this position with raffia, pulling it as tight as you can without damaging them. You can sometimes return and pull the tie a little tighter. The inside leaves, shaded by the outer ones, will slowly blanch.

Alternatively, place a large pot or box over each plant to shut out all light or cover a cloche with black plastic. Some people place a plate on the flat leaves.

Cooking

The blanched leaves have a good nutty flavour. To clean them, place the whole head face downwards in water and let it remain floating to release any soil before you finally separate the leaves.

Serve with French dressing or any type of salad cream.

Cook endive in any of the ways recommended for either chicory or lettuce.

FENNEL

Growing Florence fennel

This can be a most delicious vegetable, but unless it is well grown it can be tough and stringy. It is important to give the plants adequate room so that they will grow quickly and keep succulent.

Sow the seed in drills from April to August if you want a succession. I suggest that many sowings of short rows, one after another, is likely to result in more satisfactory crops than one long row at the same time.

Thin the seedlings to 9in apart. When you see the stalk bases swelling begin to earth them up. Generally earthing up takes place a month before the 'bulbs' are used. The earthing up not only blanches them but helps to keep them tender and succulent.

See that the plants do not suffer from drought; water them copiously in dry spells. If your soil is poor, feed them with a liquid manure from time to time.

Cooking Florence fennel

Raw Florence fennel is an excellent accompaniment to fish dishes. Finely sliced it makes a good salad on its own, although it also mixes well, particularly with yogurt, or with cream cheese blended into a vinaigrette dressing.

It is important that the 'bulbs' are young. Sometimes large bulbs have tough outer leaves. As these might be stringy it is advisable to remove them. There is no need to waste them, they can be finely shredded and cooked. Use a little lemon juice or a slice of lemon to keep them a good colour. They can also be used to flavour a bouillon for fish.

I have often made an ample serving of these outer stems by stewing them gently and then putting them in thick cream or in a bechamel sauce. Flavour and colour both of these with a few chopped fennel leaves. It is possible to string the stems just as you would string celery.

To slice the bulbs trim the root end a little. Cut the bulb in half lengthwise, then cut each half into thin slices, as thin as you can, each one with a little of the nutty root portion still attached.

These slices can be dipped into a light batter and fried crisp and brown.

Growing fennel

The perennial herb is *Foeniculum vulgare*. It is a handsome plant which reaches some 3–4ft when it is in flower. Its umbels are a mustard yellow and highly decorative.

Fennel will grow in any ordinary soil and it likes a sunny position. It is easily grown from seed, which should be sown in March. When the seedlings are large enough to handle, lift them without breaking their long tap roots and simply dibble them into the ground where they are to flower. The plants grow so large that usually two or three are sufficient. On the other hand they are so decorative that most people are tempted to grow more.

The seed can be saved and used as a spice for flavouring. But take care, if you let all the flowers go to seed you are likely to find fennel springing up everywhere in the garden.

Cooking fennel

In a mild winter you can pick fresh fennel early in February and you can have it all winter through if you cover a plant with a cloche. This is most helpful to the cook, for the leaves with their aniseed-cum-liquorice flavour are so good in all fish dishes—use it in any way suggested for parsley. Even a spoonful of the chopped herb scattered over something as ordinary as tinned mackerel will make a world of difference. Blend it into any fish paté you may make from tinned fish. I like to use it in fish soufflés and in these I also add a pinch of fennel seed.

Hard-boiled eggs are given a zest if a little fennel is used in any sauce in which they are cooked or served. It is also a good offal herb. Use a garnish of fennel if you serve kidneys with rice. Surprisingly, perhaps, fennel is good in a stuffing for roast lamb.

Grilling fish on fennel stalks is a Mediterranean method much extolled by those who love foods from that region. However, it is not so easily followed in the modern kitchen. It really is more suitable for outdoors or for one of those vast Italian kitchens complete with grill fed by long pieces of wood. But it can be done and I recommend it for some of the less delicately flavoured fish such as whiting.

Here is a recipe for a dish which approaches the flavour of fennel-grilled fish with less trouble.

Fennel Fish Flambé (serves 6)

1tsp fennel seed	salt, pepper
1tbsp fresh chopped parsley	4tbsp brandy
1tsp chopped thyme	1 large fish, say 3lb, or 6 smaller
1tsp chopped fennel	ones

Spread foil over the grill pan or dish which is to be used. Double foil is best because this does not split so easily and can be washed and used time and time again. Prepare the fish. Brush it with a little oil and sprinkle on a little salt. Grill under a medium heat for 15min on each side. Have ready a hot, strong serving dish. Transfer the fish. Have the herbs and seeds ready mixed and sprinkle them over the fish. Warm the brandy in a ladle or small pan, pour it over the fish and light it. Serve immediately.

G

GARLIC

Growing
This useful pungent vegetable is often dear to buy but it is easy to grow.
You can plant the bulbs you buy for cooking or order them from
your seedsman.

Divide the compound bulb into separate cloves and plant them 2in
deep, 4–6in apart, from February to May.

Lift the bulbs at the end of August or when the tops have died down
completely, dry and store them. I like to hang mine in ropes in a cool,
dry place.

Cooking
I know that many people say you should only bruise or squeeze garlic,
but I usually prefer to chop it very finely. When I mix it with onion
and shallot and melt them in butter, the garlic pieces seem to disappear
altogether, leaving just the flavour. It is deliciously nutty sliced finely
and browned in butter until it is crisp. My family like it this way with
liver, where 1–2 cloves are sufficient for 1lb liver.

GOOSEBERRIES

Growing
Gooseberries will grow in any good ordinary soil, but they do need
plenty of potash—sulphate of potash, not muriate which tends to cause
leaf scorch. Like the red and white currants (they are all members of
the same family, Ribes) they can be grown on two sites, sunny ones
for early crops and north or east walls for later maturing varieties.
Gooseberries are usually seen as bushes, but they can also be grown as
cordons or as standards. Like currants, if they are grown as a bush they

are best on a leg or short trunk. This means that the lowest branches are then clear of the ground which keeps the fruit clean and makes it easier to gather.

If you want large dessert fruit, then it is essential to prune all side shoots to 1in in length. But if you are more interested in lots of immature berries for pies and for bottling, then let the longer branches develop. Usually the first fruits are gathered early in June. It is then best to thin out the fruit at the same time, leaving some well-spaced berries to develop.

In any case discourage growth in the very centre of the bushes to make fruit gathering easier. Summer pruning promotes fruit bearing branches the following year. Cut side shoots to leave only 6 leaves. When mildew is a nuisance this is a good way to removing affected tips. Burn the prunings.

Bushes can take up a good deal of garden space, for they should be planted 4–6ft apart each way. As you would expect, cordons are much more economic in space. They need 1ft for singles, 1½ft for doubles and 2ft for trebles.

Cooking
One of the nicest ways to stew these berries is in a covered dish in a slow oven. For a change, sweeten them with two or three spoonfuls of honey instead of sugar.

One of my favourite ways of serving ripe gooseberries is as follows. Have ready individual dishes. Take really ripe berries after washing and draining them squeeze them into the dishes discarding the skins. You can mix these with rhubarb and make jam if you wish. Cover the fruit pulp with thin cream and sprinkle this with chopped almonds. Chill slightly and serve.

Use drained cooked gooseberries and cream to make sponge layer cakes for a delicious dinner sweet.

Summer Salad with Gooseberries

This also offers you an unusual and delicious way to use radishes. Set aside the largest ones for this purpose if you have a choice.

| 1 cup chopped, sliced or coarsely grated radish | 1 cup whole gooseberries cooked with a little sugar or honey |
| 1 cup diced cooked potato | 1tbsp chopped parsley |

Mix and serve with mayonnaise. Instead of lemon use the gooseberry liquor mixed with the olive oil and egg.

Gooseberry Sauce for Mackerel or Herrings

½lb gooseberries	1tbsp butter
2tbsp sugar	2tbsp chopped young fennel leaves
½ cup water	

Cook all together except the fennel. Simmer gently so that the gooseberries do not mash, they should be just opened. Carefully stir in the fennel just before taking the sauce from the heat.

If you have a freezer
It is easy to freeze gooseberries. Simply wash, dry and pack into bags.

HERBS

Growing

Once you have become a gardener you should be able to produce fresh herbs of some kind throughout the year. I know that dried herbs are widely used, but I cannot stress too strongly that there is a great deal of difference between the taste of fresh and the taste of dried herbs. If you are a herb-conscious cook you will know that fresh herbs can be used in abundance, whereas those that have been dried should be used with discretion or they can be very indigestible.

In my own garden I give cover to a few and others I lift and pot so that they can be forced indoors. Fortunately for me I let chervil seed itself when I first grew it and now it takes care of itself. It is at its best in winter and usually begins flowering in February. If I want chervil in summer I sow it in succession.

In mild winters parsley will grow well in any protected spot, but it can also be grown in frames or under cloches. If you lift a few plants and pot them individually in 5in pots they will make fine plants and will grow well on a window-sill.

Details of how to force herbs are given throughout this book when the herb is described under its own name.

Separate from herbs dried for cooking are those which are dried for making teas or tisanes. The method for drying is the same for all.

Gather them on a warm, sunny day. Those in flower will have the best aroma. Tie them in small bunches in separate kinds unless you are making bouquets garnis, in which case these should, traditionally, contain basil, bay leaves, thyme and sage but marjoram and tarragon are often added. If you have no bay tree the leaves can be bought by the ounce from most chemists. You can mix other herbs if you haven't all of these, but avoid mint in this collection.

Hang herb bunches in a warm, dry place, or string them from a cane wedged across your oven. Place it there when the oven is cooling. Alternatively, hang the herbs in the airing cupboard in the same way. Do not hang the bunches in the sun.

When they are dry and brittle the leaves can be rubbed from the tough stems. Do this over clean paper. Store the rubbed herbs in airtight jars clearly labelled. You can powder herbs in an electric coffee grinder. Wipe it out with a little lemon peel after each herb to remove its distinctive scent.

Another way to store dried herbs is to place each bunch in a small polythene bag. I find fresh mint, hung to dry in a bag which is tightly closed, keeps its scent and flavour extremely well when the leaves have become brittle.

Herb Teas

To make camomile tea, gather the flower heads while the yellow daisy centres are still young and bright. Spread them out on a paper or a cloth in a clean, cool and airy place to dry. When they are quite dry to the touch, store them in jars.

To make the tea, measure ½pt water into a saucepan and bring it to the boil. Throw in 1tsp camomile flowers and boil for ½min with the lid on. Remove from heat and allow to brew for a few seconds. Strain into a warmed cup. Add lemon if you wish, and honey, not sugar, as a sweetener. This is soothing when you have a headache.

Peppermint tea is good to take when you have a cold.

To make peppermint tea gather wild peppermint leaves. Use a teapot to make this, but it had better be kept specifically for peppermint tea because of the aroma. Take a handful of fresh leaves, pour on boiling water and brew for 5min under a cosy. Strain into a glass and add lemon and honey to taste. The same recipe may be used with any kind of mint.

Gather and dry leaves for winter use. Cut stems and hang or spread them out to dry. When they are brittle to the touch strip the leaves from the stems and store them in airtight jars. Make the tea as directed for camomile.

Herb Vinegars

You can use just one herb—tarragon is a favourite—or you can mix several. Mint vinegar will be delicious with cold mutton. Sage with pork, basil with tomatoes. Garlic vinegar is good too.

In general the method for making herb vinegars is as follows. Gather young leaves and, without squeezing them, wash them. Dry them on a towel or thick kitchen tissue. Pack a preserving jar half full of leaves. Boil some vinegar (wine or cider vinegar is best) and pour it over the leaves until the jar is full. Cover tightly. After two weeks or so strain the vinegar through a square of damp cloth or through a thick paper towel until it is quite clear. Bottle and cork and label clearly.

Quick Herb Loaf

My family insist on calling this 'your bread', but it is really a large scone shaped into a loaf or into small loaves or rolls, and baked quickly.

Set the oven at about 450° F, 230° C, and collect a pastry bowl, board, brush and greased baking sheet. Weigh the flour, chop the fresh herbs and collect the other ingredients:

1lb self-raising flour	to add a little sage and savory
1oz butter or lard	to the mixture
1tsp salt	¾pt milk
1tbsp any fresh herbs, but I like	poppy seeds

Empty the flour and salt into the basin, but reserve a little flour for later on. Rub in the fat and the herbs. Begin stirring in the milk, using a palette knife. The dough should be moist enough for it to stick to your hands. Keep them well floured and work quickly. Cover the pastry board with flour. Tip the dough on to this, scrape the bowl well, and quickly shape the dough into a long loaf. Alternatively, cut it into roll portions. Slash the top of the loaf with a sharp knife, making deep cuts in the top. Paint with milk. Sprinkle on the poppy seeds. Bake for about 30min or until the bread sounds firm when you lift it and tap the base. Serve it before it completely cools. The crust is best then.

Herb and garlic butter with cheese go well with this bread, and if you serve soup first you will find it filling enough for a meal, especially for the young, who seem to be able to consume vast quantities of starch.

If you have a deep freeze and buy meat in quantity, you are likely to have certain odds and ends to use. Unless you make the most of these your bulk buy will not prove to be much of a saving. Here is a supper dish which I make from a pig's trotter and knuckle end combined with a beef marrow bone.

Green Brawn

Simmer together the trotter and the beef bones for some hours. Just cover them with water, and to this add a bay leaf, crushed juniper berries, bouquet garni, a shallot, onion and clove of garlic, a stick of celery or lovage and some salt. When the stock is really thick and the trotter tender, strain all through a colander. Skim off any fat. Set the stock aside and extract as much meat as possible from the trotter and bones. Scoop out the marrow, cut up any gelatinous material but discard gristle. Place this in a 1pt soufflé dish. Have ready a good bunch of mixed green herbs. Wash, dry and chop these and add them to the meat mixture. I like to add also about a dozen or so pistachio nuts.

Taste the stock and adjust the seasoning. Brawns usually need plenty. I always add a good dash of Worcestershire sauce and freshly ground pepper and 1tsp lemon juice. Pour the stock over this mixture so that the level comes to just below the rim of the dish. Place this in the refrigerator to set. To serve, cut the brawn into slices, serve with vinaigrette sauce. It makes a good first course.

HORSERADISH

Growing

There is no comparison between a sauce made with freshly grated horseradish and one which is bought ready bottled. There is though one great problem about growing this plant; if you leave it alone it is extremely invasive and a bed will soon spread through the garden and the plants will become inferior in quality.

The best thing to do is to treat it like many other crops and plant it anew each year. Lift the roots in November and store them in dry sand. Use the largest and save the smallest to replant the following March.

These root cuttings need to be about 3in long. When you cut them mark tip and tail by slanting one end. Plant them a foot apart with the tips just under the soil. Any ordinary soil will do, but it must be deep, enriched and easily worked.

Cooking

One of my vivid childhood memories is of going to visit one of my grandmothers who lived in south-east London and on Sunday morning being sent down to the nearby street market to buy horseradish. This was always sold by the same woman, who stood on the edge of the pavement with a few roots spread out on a piece of newspaper which she held out before her. I asked for a 'pennorth' and was given one or two thick roots. It was then my job to peel and grate the roots, and I remember so clearly the acrid scent as they were scraped and the hot, exciting taste when eaten with roast beef.

The sauce was made very simply. It was mixed with cream and a little salt. It had to be thick enough to be spooned out. It was always served cold.

Apple and Horseradish Sauce for Fish

This is especially good for mackerel. Mix:

4tbsp grated horseradish	1tsp lemon juice
4tbsp apple purée	$\frac{3}{4}$pt cream

Don't hesitate to use horseradish in salads, but blend it with something contrasting such as carrot which is sweeter and not pungent, or celery.

Ox Tongue with Horseradish Sauce (serves 4)

2oz grated horseradish	1 or 2 egg yolks
$\frac{1}{2}$pt stock	salt and pepper
1tbsp melted butter	$\frac{1}{2}$tsp mustard mixed in a little
4tbsp cream	vinegar
1tbsp breadcrumbs	

Boil the horseradish and stock together, simmering gently for 20min. Remove from heat and add butter, cream and breadcrumbs. Replace the pan on the heat and let it simmer as you stir it well until it thickens. Strain the sauce through a sieve. Beat the egg yolks and add, together with the seasoning and the mustard.

Have ready the slices of ox tongue arranged in a shallow oven dish made really hot. Pour the sauce over these and serve.

KOHLRABI

Growing
Here is a vegetable which plays a dual role. The roots, really the swollen bases of the leaf stems, can be cooked in one way and the leaves in another.

Sow in shallow drills in April and May and onwards in succession. Thin out to 6–9in apart.

Cooking
You can cook the roots in the same way as turnips and celeriac.

Kohlrabi with Pork

1lb belly of pork diced	white wine and good white
1lb peeled and sliced kohlrabi	stock
bacon dripping or butter	seasoning, bay leaf, parsley
1 good sized onion, finely	
chopped	

Melt the fat in a saucepan. Add the chopped onion and cook but do not brown. Add the kohlrabi. Coat the slices with the fat and onion. Put in the pork. Barely cover with equal amounts of white wine and stock. Add a bay leaf, seasoning and simmer until all is tender. Sprinkle with parsley to serve.

Kohlrabi Complete (serves 4)

8 kohlrabi with leaves	2tbsp flour
2tbsp good dripping or butter	

Cut off leaves, peel roots. Slice the latter and cook in boiling salted water until just tender. Meanwhile boil the greens, also in salted water. Both should take 10–15min. Drain both. Arrange the sliced roots in the centre of a heatproof dish. Chop the greens finely and arrange them in a ring around the sliced roots. Cover and keep warm while you make a sauce by melting the fat, blending in the flour and pouring into this ½pt of the kohlrabi water. When thick and smooth pour this over the vegetables and serve.

If you have a freezer
Pick off the stems if these seem too long and tough and blanch the leaves for 2min. Peel and slice the roots, and blanch for 2min.

L

LEEKS

Growing

The important thing is to sow leeks thinly so that the plants can stay where they have been sown until you have space to transplant them to their final quarters.

Sow from early March to mid-April in a prepared seed bed. Transplant when they are about 6in high or more. Leeks are planted differently from any other vegetable. Make really deep holes with a dibber, 9in apart and as deep as the plants and drop each one into the hole. The tip of the leaves should just reach the top of the hole. Pour a little water into each hole. From there you can leave it to the wind and the rain to cover the roots. The plant will swell and finally fill the hole.

I have had best results by filling each hole after planting, with good moss peat. Rows I treat this way grow faster and better than the others.

During the summer and autumn draw the earth up the stems to blanch them. Leeks are hardy and can be left in the ground all winter and dug as required.

Cooking

First make sure the leeks are perfectly clean. Cut off the white portion, slice down the centre to within 1in of the base, wash under the tap or leave soaking until all the grit has been removed.

Don't waste the green portions. Wash these well, bunch and slice across finely. Bring to the boil in water or stock and simmer slowly until they are quite tender. This takes longer with old leaves. Cool, then sieve or blend. You now have a purée which, when thinned with stock or vegetable water or milk, makes an excellent soup. If you mix some with a thick purée of spinach you can make a tasty flan or soufflé.

Leeks à la Vinaigrette

I like to serve these as a first course. Cook the white part of the leeks, in sufficient boiling salted water to cover them, until tender but still firm and shapely. Drain them thoroughly and cover with French dressing while still warm. Serve cold.

Leeks and potatoes go well together.

Normandy Potatoes

1lb potatoes peeled and thinly sliced	bouquet garni of bay leaf, thyme, 2 sage leaves
4 average-size leeks sliced	½ cup (¼pt) white stock
3tbsp chopped parsley	2–3oz butter
seasoning	

Wash the potato slices, drain and dry. This removes surplus starch. Place alternate layers of potatoes and leeks in a buttered oven dish, sprinkle each layer with parsley and seasoning as you go. Finish with a layer of potatoes. Put in the bouquet garni, dab butter over the surface and pour in stock. Bring to the boil on the stove and either continue to simmer the dish there or finish off in a moderate oven, 350° F, 180° C.

If you serve the dish as a complete meal and not as a vegetable, top it with grated cheese and brown it under the grill once the potatoes are tender.

I cannot give you exact timings as different potatoes take longer to cook than others, but 30min on the stove and 1hr in the oven would be about right.

Vichyssoise (serves 4)

This is one of the most famous and delicious blendings of potatoes and leeks:

3 medium leeks, white portion only	4 cups (2pt) chicken stock
1 medium onion	1-2 cups cream
2tbsp butter	chopped chives (essential)
4 medium potatoes	salt and pepper

Slice, chop finely, or mince the leeks and the onion. Put them in a pan with the butter, cover and soften but do not brown. Add the potatoes, peeled and finely sliced or grated. Add the stock. Simmer all together until the potatoes are quite tender. Sieve or blend them to a smooth liquid. Add salt and pepper. When cold stir in cream and chill. Serve very cold in individual bowls. Sprinkle the surface of the soup with chopped chives.

If you have a freezer
Don't bother to freeze leeks, they lose their flavour. Yet they retain it in Vichyssoise. I have a friend who freezes a gallon at a time, all in individual cartons, as a first course for unexpected guests.

LETTUCE

Growing
You can have succulent salad lettuce the year round, for there are many varieties other than the summer types, some of them hardy enough to stand the winter outdoors in mild districts.

There is also a loose-leaf lettuce, Salad Bowl, which can be picked leaf by leaf and which is ideal for very small gardens because you need only a few plants. I have found this will stand the winter under cloches.

For summer or winter you can also have both cos and cabbage types, although for the summer the crisphead types like the large Webb's Wonderful are gradually ousting the long cos. The cabbage types have yellow hearts and the crisphead varieties are white.

You can make the first sowings of summer types outdoors in March and can continue sowing every 2 weeks until July. In August and early September you should begin sowing winter lettuce. For spring salads you can sow suitable varieties in the greenhouse in January and February, prick these off into boxes when large enough to handle and finally plant them out under cloches during March. You can also sow lettuce broadcast in frames in early October and use these for transplanting under glass or cloches from February onwards.

Seed should be sown thinly in shallow drills and rows should be 1ft apart. If you broadcast seed in frames cover it with a thin surface of moist peat.

Cooking

I use the thinnings of both lettuce and spinach and cook them together. They need to be well washed and to have their tiny roots picked off.

Sometimes I cook a kind of hot salad by using all the few 'firsts'. For instance, thinnings from a row of lettuce, a green onion rushing to flower, the first and only courgette ready to cut, the first few peas and beans. These all go together in a heavy pan with a good handful of roughly chopped parsley, just enough water to cover the base of the pan and 1tbsp olive oil, butter or margarine. They are brought to the boil and simmered slowly for 10–15min then strained and served. Delicious and rare!

I also use lettuce in some recipes which call for green peppers, the slightly bitter taste of both vegetables is similar enough to pass without notice. To do this successfully the lettuce, fresh or frozen, must be shredded very finely so that it becomes really tender and amalgamates well with the other ingredients and the dish cooked slowly (see Green Beans in Casserole).

Lettuce can be cooked in any way recommended for both endive and chicory.

Braised lettuce is the basis of many fine French dishes. When I cook lettuce as a green I do it this way.

Cooked Lettuce with Onion

Allow ½ medium-sized onion, and 1 whole lettuce per person. If you are using thinnings, use a good handful instead of one head. Wash well and cut the onion roughly. Put these in a pan together with a good handful of roughly chopped parsley, 1tbsp olive oil or butter and salt to taste. Just cover the bottom of the pan with water, no more. Bring to the boil slowly and simmer until tender. Drain and either serve whole or chop.

If you have a freezer
Freeze lettuce hearts in the same way as I recommended for cabbage but without the apple. Braised lettuces are much appreciated for winter meals. Try shredding them finely and mixing with equal quantities of tomato—frozen or tinned. Simmer slowly and for a long time so that much of the moisture evaporates. Taste and season. Serve with meat and rice.

LOVAGE

Growing
This herb seems to have fallen from favour in recent years, which is a pity, for it is a useful plant for any gardener-cook to have in the herb patch. Its value lies largely in its strong celery flavour, which means that it can fill a gap when celery and celeriac are out of season.

Lovage is a perennial which grows 2ft tall. It prefers a rich, moist soil.

Cooking
Use the leaves and stems to give celery flavour to soups, sauces and court bouillons.

M

MARJORAM

Growing (see Herbs)

Marjoram is an important ingredient in Italian dishes. The botanical name for the common or 'pot' marjoram is *Origanum onites* and for the sweet or knotted marjoram is *Origanum majorana*. Oregano is the wild Mediterranean marjoram.

The first is a hardy perennial which will grow in any ordinary soil although it does need a sunny place. It is an attractive plant whose 1ft high stems become smothered with dull purple flowers. It grows quite easily from seed which should be sown outdoors in March. Transplant the seedlings as soon as they are large enough to handle. Pot a few at the same time so that you can force them in winter.

Sweet or knotted marjoram is more tender and so, although it is a perennial, it is more usually treated as an annual. It can be grown in pots indoors, or it can be sown indoors in March and planted out in April. This marjoram likes a richer soil than the other and sun is essential.

Cooking

This is one of the bouquet garni herbs. Marjoram is also one of those used in mixed or 'sweet' herbs sold in packets.

The young leaves of the sweet or knotted marjoram bring a pleasant pungency to salads and the flavour is just right when the salad is served with cold or hot meats, especially lamb and pork.

I like to sprinkle the herb on beef before it is roasted and I always use it in beef stews and casseroles.

Use marjoram with any of the pastas and in most Italian dishes, with tomatoes and fish, especially shell fish.

MARROWS

Growing

Marrows, melons, squash, cucumbers, pumpkins and gourds all belong to the same family. The edible kinds include some which are lovely to look at, varieties of *Cucurbita maxima, moschata* and *pepo*. Among them are the gay and delicious Turk's cap gourds, which look like orange and green turbans. In Britain, generally speaking, we reserve the name 'gourds' for the ornamental kinds grown for decoration, but there are also many edible kinds which are gourds or gourd-like. The prettily shaped custard marrow, crook-neck, gem and orange squash, for instance, are as attractive to look at as they are tasty to eat.

Plants grow best on level ground where their roots do not become dry as they do when grown on individual mounds as is sometimes suggested. Give them good, really rich soil. I always make their 'stations' warm and snug at the roots by using plenty of fresh grass mowings to make a small hot bed. To do this remove the soil from a circle roughly $1\frac{1}{2}$–2ft wide and a spit (the depth of a spade) deep. Fill this with grass, trample down well and cover with the soil which was removed and into which a generous handful or two of Plus or some other good general fertiliser has been incorporated. Depress the centre of this area slightly and either plant or sow seeds directly at this point. Seeds germinate best if a little cover, a glass jar, plastic cage, cloche or some other kind of transparent covering is put over them.

Sow in May, three seeds to a station, and thin out to one bush or two trailing types. Guard against slugs. Although the soil will settle as the grass consolidates, the depression will remain and will hold the moisture without which the young plants will not grow quickly. Water well in dry spells.

Alternatively, in April in a heated frame, greenhouse or on a sunny window-sill, sow the seed singly in pots, each in a 3in pot, the seed on its edge as you push it in to bury it. When the plants have outgrown this size pot, move them on to the next size. Do not let them become pot bound.

Bush types should be grown about 3–4ft apart and trailers as much as 6ft unless they are climbing. When they are trailing along the ground you can use canes stuck into the ground on each side of the trails to train them to go the way you want.

All kinds and varieties can be used very young, like courgettes, when they will need neither peeling nor seeding. The plant will keep producing more flowers if you have given it rich soil and keep it watered during dry spells. Some people take the trouble to fertilise the flowers taking the pollen from the males to the females, which are distinguishable because they have the tiny fruit below the flower.

If you want to store any for winter, wait until they are really ripe, with wood-hard skins.

Cooking

To prepare a ripe marrow with hard skin, place it in the oven until it softens. After this cut it through lengthwise and remove the seeds and the stringy centre with a large spoon. The golden flesh can then be scooped and scraped away from the skin, mashed, blended with butter or margarine and reheated in a pan. Season to taste. Some people like nutmeg instead of pepper.

If you want to make a few apples go a long way use marrow to eke them out in a pie. Marrow used this way is not so very different from pumpkin which makes a wonderful pie. Use 1lb marrow to ½lb of apples. The flavour is vastly improved and the pie lifted out of the ordinary class if you add to this mixture 2oz raisins and the juice of a lemon. Use a little of the zest of the lemon sprinkled over the mixture before you add the pastry. Add sugar to taste just as you would in an ordinary apple pie.

Fried Marrow

Use young marrow, clean but do not peel. Cut through in ½in thick slices. Dip them in flour, tap off the surplus and fry in hot bacon dripping.

Marrow Jam

This is a basic recipe for jams of any of these vegetables when really ripe.

Peel and seed. Weigh the pulp and juice. For every 2lb pulp use 1½lb of preserving sugar and the juice of 1 lemon.

First put the sugar in the preserving pan and add ¾pt water. Let it dissolve and then boil slowly for 5min. Skim if necessary. Pour in the pulp, stir well, boil slowly and skim if necessary until the jam reaches the jelly stage. Pour into hot jars.

You can use stored, ripe marrow in any way recommended later for squash.

MINT

Growing

Most widely known of the mints is the smooth spearmint or lamb's mint. This is the type that is forced out of season and sold for mint sauce and new potatoes. But it really is not the best for these purposes. Much the better flavoured is the woolly or apple mint. This is a taller plant than the spearmint and stronger growing altogether. I prefer to use this one in mint sorbets and mint-flavoured jellies. Peppermint also can be used for this sweet.

Most mints can be used in the kitchen. Pennyroyal, seldom used today, was once popular for all dishes made from pig's offal and for stuffings for pork. It was considered to be a herb which aided digestion.

Mints do best in a rich, moist soil. If your herb garden is only a small one you should control the mint in some way because it is very invasive. One of the best ways is to plant it in a bottomless bucket or very strong plastic bag or cannister and then to bury this container in the herb border with its rim just above ground. If you bury the rim the mint roots will creep over the soil. Lift the container every 3 or 4 years and divide and renew the mint.

If you allow mint to go naturally to flower it will become unproductive early in the year. On the other hand, if you keep cutting the tips only, side shoots will develop. Cut alternate plants down to ground level in June. These will soon shoot again. It should be possible to go on cutting fresh mint until well into the late autumn. To force mint for winter, lift some roots any time between October and May, plant them in shallow boxes or pots and grow them on a warm window-sill or in a greenhouse.

Cooking

You can prepare delicious mint jelly to serve with meat in place of mint sauce by using some of the sour fruits from the garden. Windfall apples, rhubarb or gooseberries can be boiled with a little water and sieved or blended and put through a jelly bag. To each 1pt juice add 1lb sugar and a good bunch of mint. Boil and test. When the liquid jellies remove the mint and pour the liquid into hot jars. Tie down while hot. I suggest that you use small jars, just enough for one meal, otherwise you may find that some is wasted.

Orange Mint Sauce

The jelly can be used to make an excellent orange-flavoured sauce for a roast joint of lamb. Remove the joint and put it on to a hot dish and keep it warm. Drain off the fat from the baking tin taking care to retain the juices in the pan. Tip in roughly 1 cup mint jelly and as it melts mix in all the meat juices until they are blended. Have ready the peel from an orange, finely sliced. To do this most easily wash the orange and peel with a potato peeler and then cut the peel into fine strips. I find it quickest to make a bunch of strips of the peel and to slice through the layers. When the jelly is melted pour the sauce off into a smaller vessel (I use a saucepan-cum-sauce boat) bring it to the boil, add the orange rinds, let it simmer for a while so that the peel becomes less opaque, and serve.

N

NASTURTIUMS

Growing

The plants commonly known as nasturtiums (*Tropaeolum majus* and *nanum*) are pretty flowering plants, with a taste rather like watercress. The true botanical nasturtium (*N. officinale*) is, it happens, a watercress.

Nasturtiums will grow in most soils, but will flower best where the soil is poor, so if you want the plants for salad only give them a site that is rich and leaves will predominate at the expense of flowers. You can, of course, grow the plants for the dual purpose of providing both food and flower.

Sow the seeds 1in deep where they are to grow. Thin them out by transplanting those which are too thick.

Keep the seed pods picked off if you want to keep the blooms going until autumn. If you want to pickle the seeds pick them when they are young and green.

Cooking

Use the leaves like any other salad crop. They are delicious in sandwiches. Use buds and half-open flowers to garnish dishes. Chop seeds and mix them with yogurt for a spicy, creamy salad dressing. Use them raw in curries. Throw a few seeds in at the last minute.

Pickled Nasturtium Seeds, or False Capers

To each 1pt vinegar add 1oz salt, 6 peppercorns and a bay leaf.

Gather the seeds when they are dry. Clean them by rubbing them in a cloth or kitchen paper. Pack them into the jars and pour the vinegar and spices over them.

The longer you keep this pickle the better it will be.

ONIONS

Growing

It is both possible and cheap to grow onions from seed sown in open ground. I do this but I also make great use of onion sets, which mature quicker and can be harvested much earlier. These are tiny onion bulbs whose growth has been arrested. They were grown from seed the previous year, ripened prematurely, lifted and stored. They begin growing again almost as soon as they are planted in March.

I find that it is best to plant them in shallow drills so that the tops of the bulbs are just under the soil surface. Draw the soil back into the drill and around the sets. As they grow they will gradually pull themselves above the soil as they should be. As you hand weed (do not use a hoe along onion rows in case you damage the bulbs and leave open wounds for pests and diseases to penetrate) you can help by pulling the soil away from them should this be necessary. Plant them 1–2in apart.

The shoots soon elongate and the little bulbs grow fast and become fleshy. As soon as they begin to touch I begin pulling them for cooking or salads.

In some seasons some of the bulbs may send up flower stalks. You can detect these quite easily; they are strong central stems topped with a little club which grows larger as the globe of flowers develops inside the sheath. At the same time the base of the tough stem swells. Pick off the flower top and leave the bulb to grow. In this case it is almost certain to divide, and one or two small onions will develop around the stem. These will not be suitable for storing but they can be kept for a few weeks. I prefer to pull out these 'bolters'. The tough central stem is consigned to the stock pot as flavour while the rest of the green is cooked.

Onion seed should be sown thinly and also thinned out later. The thinnings are spring or salad or bunch onions. The exception to thin sowing is when you wish to grow pickle onions. There are special varieties for this. Let these grow unthinned so that they remain small. These are also the perfect tiny onions to cook with peas, French style, with dishes like coq au vin, and use with gherkins.

Sow seeds in March and April and also in August for the following year. These late sowings produce the true spring onion and I have sown them successfully as late as mid-September. It is best to leave these rows unthinned, for one plant helps to protect the other. If you do not want to pull spring onions you can leave the plants to mature.

Onions need good soil. Remember that their roots go deep. Dress the soil with lime early in February and again before you sow. If for some reason you can't do this, sprinkle the soil well with lime after sowing. Always tread the soil lightly after sowing, as onions need firm soil.

You can begin thinning as soon as the plants are large enough to handle. I am not a traditionalist over onion growing. I wait and thin them when the thinnings themselves are large enough to use, then I thin as I do every other root crop, going over the rows continually pulling alternate plants, until finally there are roots big enough to grow or to lift and store.

Cooking

Don't waste your onions by leaving them all to grow big and to ripen. Green tops, scallions, give a fine flavour to many dishes. Make a savoury white sauce this way.

Take about a handful of onions. You need ½ cup when they are all thinly sliced, but proportions are not all that important in this case. Gently melt them in a covered pan with 1tbsp butter. Add a finely chopped clove of garlic if liked. When all are tender stir in 1 heaped tbsp flour and blend. Slowly add either ½pt milk (it mixes quicker if it is hot) or some vegetable water, in which case you may not need to add salt. You can use this sauce as a base for certain dishes. If you tip a tin of salmon and a good amount of chopped parsley into it you have American wiggle, which should be served on toast. I use it as a basis for soufflé. I add 4 eggs, a small tin of fish such as pilchards, shrimps, tunny, and lots of fresh green herbs.

Baked onions are another simple and delicious way of cooking onions.

Here is a good and simple supper dish which you can adjust to feed any number of people. Hard boil eggs and halve them. Lay them on the base of a shallow, buttered baking dish. Pour the sauce over them so that they are just covered. Cover the surface with grated cheese and a good sprinkling of nutmeg. Grill and serve. For something a little more substantial, stir in a small tin of fish, some sliced smoked sausage, mushrooms or meat left overs. Cover the eggs in the same way. Toast goes well with this dish.

Onion Starters (serves 4)

4 onions ⎫ finely chopped 1 clove garlic, ⎭ 1tbsp melted butter 1tbsp flour ½tsp salt freshly ground pepper to taste	nutmeg ½ cup (¼pt) thin cream or evaporated milk ¼ cup white breadcrumbs 1 egg 1tbsp mixed fines herbes

Chop the garlic finely. Put it in with the chopped onions and the butter and cook all together until tender but not browned. Stir in the flour and seasoning, blend. Add the cream or milk and blend, then add the breadcrumbs. Cook until the mixture thickens. Draw pan from the fire and cool slightly. Stir in the egg yolk and the herbs. Beat the egg white until stiff and fold into the mixture. Divide the mixture into four buttered ramekins. Sprinkle with nutmeg. Bake for ½hr in a moderate oven, 350° F, 180° C.

P

PARSLEY

Growing

Not everyone knows that there is a fine dual-purpose parsley, Hamburg, or parsnip-rooted. Its roots are extremely tender and succulent and can be cooked and eaten just like parsnips; indeed, I sometimes think that they are far superior to them. The leaves have a distinctive flavour, but they are not 'moss curled'.

Sow this parsley in March in shallow drills 12in apart and thin the plants to 4–6in apart. Lift the roots in October and onwards, although you can pick the leaves as soon as these are large enough. It is best to store the roots if you live where winters are hard.

The other variety, moss-curled parsley, is usually sown twice, once in spring for summer use and also from June to August. The spring-sown crop will continue growing quite well if you keep picking it but if you want to lift some roots to grow in a frame for fresh parsley in winter, it is best to sow again in summer.

This herb does best in semi-shaded sites, in ordinary but well-manured soil. The seeds take 6–8 weeks to germinate, so sow some radish with them to indicate their location.

Cooking

To keep parsley for a few days wash, dry well and store in an airtight container in a cool place. If it has been chopped, wrap it in a piece of kitchen paper before putting it in the container and this will absorb the juices.

If you want to dry parsley first wash and then dry it and spread it in a thin layer on a rack. Place this in a slow oven, as low a temperature as possible, and allow it to dry slowly. When the leaves feel brittle, rub them between your fingers and store the 'powder' in an airtight jar.

Fried Parsley

This makes an attractive garnish but it is also good to eat. It is important that the parsley is quite dry, otherwise it will splutter violently when put into the fat. It is as well to wash and dry it some hours in advance. Pat it dry on a kitchen tissue and then let it finish in the air.

Use a frying basket and get the fat really hot with a blue haze rising from it. Lower the parsley in the basket. The fat will hiss alarmingly! When the noise stops remove the basket and drain the parsley on kitchen paper. The bright green sprigs will keep crisp for some minutes.

Parsley roots are edible and fully flavoured. Wash them well, cut in rings and use to flavour soups. If you cut them thinly enough you can dry them in the same way as the leaves.

If you have a freezer
Wash, dry and fill a container with the sprigs. Press them down well.

When you want to use the parsley you may find it easiest merely to grate the block. It will be too limp when thawed to fry, but it will flavour soups and sauces. If you chop it first, it loses its flavour in the freezer.

PARSNIPS

Growing
Sow parsnips early, in March, as soon as the ground is dry enough to draw shallow drills. Make these 12–15in apart. The seed takes a long time to germinate but you can sow radish in the same row. Thin the plants to 3in apart then, when the roots are as large as a small carrot, pull alternate roots and use them for flavouring. Let the others remain to mature. You can either lift all or half the crop in November and store the roots. Alternatively, in all but frosty weather you can lift when required. Use before the following March or the plants will run to seed.

Long-rooted varieties are most often grown, but the intermediates are best for shallow soils. I always sow more parsnips in July and lift them young. They really are very good grown this way, and an intermediate variety is most suitable.

Cooking

Freshly lifted roots never take so long to cook as those which have been stored. Scrub, rather than peel them, cut into rings ½–1in thick, or slice into halves or quarters, put into just enough boiling water to cover them, and cook for 10–15min. Serve with melted butter into which a generous handful of chervil or parsley has been stirred.

Parsnips roasted around the joint are top favourites with my family. The parsnips are parboiled. They are then placed around or under the joint and turned two or three times during cooking so that all the outer surface becomes really brown and crisp from the fat and gravy.

You can make good parsnip chips. Children like these, Parboil the roots, cut into chips and fry in deep fat.

Parsnip Scallops (serves 4)

This makes a good starter to a meal. Serve it in deep scallop shells or individual dishes.

½ cup mashed parsnip
1 egg
1oz butter
1tbsp cream
1tsp chopped fennel or 2tsp
    chopped chervil or parsley,
    but the first is best

1 pinch cumin seed
seasoning, lemon juice, nutmeg,
    Worcestershire sauce and a
    dash of curry powder
½ cup flaked fish or tinned fish of
    a bland kind such as tunny

Butter the shells or dishes. Beat the egg and cream together, add the parsnips and continue beating. Add lemon juice, herbs and seasoning. Stir in the fish. Divide the mixture between the dishes, put a knob of butter on each, sprinkle with nutmeg and bake in a hot oven.

Parsnip Fritters

This is an excellent way of using left-overs.

1 cup mashed parsnip	gill milk
1 egg	1tsp Worcestershire sauce
good pinch salt	2tsp chopped parsley
1oz butter	wholemeal flour for coating
2tbsp flour	

Beat the egg well, add the parsnip and continue beating until the mixture is light. Stir in the other ingredients and if the mixture seems too stiff add another tablespoon of milk. Spread it on a floured plate. When it is cold, divide equally and shape into rolls. Dust your hands well with flour to do this. Lightly dust the fritters with flour. Using a basket fry them in deep fat. Alternatively fry them in a shallow pan in butter, in which case flatten the cakes. Fry one side and then the other.

Parsnip Wine

4lb parsnips	1 orange
1gal water	3lb white sugar
1tsp ground ginger	yeast
2 lemons	

Scrub the parsnips but do not peel them. Cut them into $\frac{1}{4}$–$\frac{1}{2}$in slices. Boil them in 1gal water with the ground ginger and rinds of the lemons and orange until the parsnips are just tender. Place sugar in bucket and strain the parsnip liquid over it. Stir and leave to cool. When lukewarm, add the citrus juices and prepared yeast. Cover closely and leave for 24hr. Pour the liquid or must into a jar. Insert an airlock and leave to ferment. When all fermentation has ceased, rack off into bottles, cork and store.

Just one point of interest: there is no need to waste the parsnips. They can be roasted.

If you have a freezer
Although parsnips store well it is sometimes useful to freeze them—for instance, in early spring if you want to clear the remains of a crop, or if you have a lot left over from making wine. The last simply need putting into containers because they are already cooked.

Otherwise, scrub, peel, slice or dice. Blanch for 2min and pack with some headroom.

PEARS

Growing
Pears ripen according to variety, the earliest being ready to pick in July. Those which ripen during winter have to be picked when they are ready to leave the tree and stored.

Pears are much longer lived than apples, although they are not, perhaps, such a useful fruit. They grow best on slightly acid soil. On alkaline soils they tend to suffer from iron deficiency. This can be corrected fairly easily these days, but often the cost of something like Sequestrene might outweigh the value of the fruit crop. These things have to be taken into account.

Plenty of well-rotted dung applied as a top dressing and very carefully forked into the top 2in of the soil will act as a useful source of food and will also help to maintain the acidity of the soil.

Bush, pyramid, espalier, fan and cordon-trained pears are less demanding of garden space than standard trees. Only a few varieties are unsuited to this type of training. I much admire the way that pears and some other fruits are grown in Switzerland, where a row is planted along a path running around a house. These are then trained cordonwise and tied to a supporting iron framework. They are taken up to about 7ft, bent at right angles and then taken over to the side of the house, thus forming a roof or arbour over the path.

Walls of a house also offer a fine place for espaliers and fan-trained pairs. South-, west- or east-facing walls or fences will do. Quickripening varieties can go on north walls. The espaliers are sometimes used at the sides of a garden path, especially in kitchen gardens. They can also be grown as pergolas and look very beautiful when in blossom.

Cooking

All dessert pears can be cooked. Usually the more delicious a pear is when raw, the better it is when stewed or bottled. Immature pears are often very hard and take hours to cook. When cooked they deepen in colour. One of the best ways to deal with pears that take a long time to soften is to bake them in a covered pot in the oven while you are cooking some other dish that needs several hours.

I like to use nearly ripe pears finely sliced in salads. They seem to go especially well with ham and some fish, just as melon does.

Chocolate Cream Pears (serves 8)

This is a good recipe for bottled pears.

1 2lb jar of bottled pears, roughly diced	1 small knob of butter
8oz cooking or plain chocolate	2tsp fine sugar
½pt double cream	2tsp finely ground coffee
2oz almonds	1tbsp brandy

Blanch the almonds by putting them in a bowl and pouring boiling water over them. Leave them for a minute and then skin them. Put them in a small pan with unsalted butter and gently fry them until brown, or put them with the butter in a dish under the grill. In either case keep turning them so that they are browned all over. Put them on kitchen paper to degrease them and then chop fairly coarsely.

Divide the pears among 8 individual glasses or bowls. Grate the chocolate finely and mix it with the coffee and sugar. Begin to whip the cream, and at the same time add the chocolate mixture little by little. Just before the cream mixture thickens stir in the brandy.

Divide the cream topping among the glasses and pile it on top of the pears. Sprinkle the almonds on the cream.

Pear Ketchup

Use good cooking pears for this. Stew them in the ordinary way but with only water enough to cover and no sugar. When they are really tender mash them. A potato masher is good for this, and then either sieve or liquidise them in an electric mixer. To every 1qt pears add:

I cup sugar	½tsp black pepper
½ cup (¼pt) vinegar	½tsp ground cinnamon
Itsp salt	½tsp ground cloves

Mix all the ingredients and boil them slowly until the liquid thickens, stirring occasionally. Pour into warm jars and seal well.

Serve with cold meats and cheese.

Pear Wine

For this you will need really ripe pears, even sleepy fruits will do. You can also use any peel and cores left over after bottling pears.

Igal chopped pears	ferment on their own but
Igal water	modern wine makers seem to
3lb sugar to each Igal juice	prefer to use yeast)
wine yeast (the pears should	

Soak the pears in the water. Cover, opening only to stir daily for a fortnight. Strain and measure. Add 3lb sugar to each gallon. Add prepared yeast, stir and cover. When fermentation takes place, usually in 2 days, pour into a jar and insert airlock. Bottle when fermentation ceases.

PEAS

Growing

Frozen peas really are wonderful value for money, but I think that once you have gathered your own peas you will always yearn for their special flavour and texture. This greatly compensates for any work involved.

Peas are attractive plants which will blend in well with decorative plants—they look unattractive only in their very last stages. A really pretty pea plant is the tall purple-podded variety which has green peas. These are round and mealy and make excellent fresh green pea soup. A mangetout variety of sugar pea, Dwarf de Grace, has pretty lavender-coloured blooms and sweet tender pods.

Traditionally gardeners sow 3 crops of ordinary peas throughout spring and summer—early, main crop and late—and you can go on sowing them until late June or July. The sequence of sowing is as follows: early varieties in March, if the weather is right; more can be sown as this crop appears above the ground; main crop and late croppers sow in late April and May. Use early varieties for late sowing. If you have a sheltered garden, or alternatively cloches, you can sow the hardy round-seeded varieties in November. These will stand the winter out of doors and produce an early crop. Round-seeded peas are not so sweet as the wrinkled types.

Sow peas in double or treble rows in a drill 6–9in wide and 3in deep. I find it easiest to remove the soil with a small spade. I place a layer of well-moistened peat along the base of the drill and sow the seeds on this, 3in apart each way. A ½pt of seed should sow 30ft. Cover with soil and then lightly tread along the row to compact the soil. But don't overdo this.

Dwarf varieties will grow without sticks, but all do best with supports. These can be the most expensive part of a pea crop. In the days when woods were coppiced there was always a good supply of hazel twigs, which are ideal for this purpose. Less expensive nowadays, because you can go on using them year after year, are bamboos set 6in apart along each side of the row and strung together with strong black cotton or thread. Begin near to the ground, as this will also keep the birds off. Other methods I have used are small-mesh wire netting placed tent-wise along the row; narrow wire netting stood upright along each side supported by canes; and plastic-covered wire garden edging, which I think is likely to last for ever, and is simply and easily pushed into the ground on each side of the rows.

If you want to grow several rows of peas, space them according to their height 2ft high peas should be grown 2ft apart. Lettuce, radish or any other quick-maturing crop can be grown between them so long as it is out of the way when you have to gather the peas.

Cooking
My tip for always having sweet-tasting peas is to cook a small onion with them. Cut the onion in four, put it in salted water, bring it to the boil and add the peas. The sugar from the onion will sweeten the peas and they will also retain their colour. I use this method for cooking most green vegetables. It is particularly good for the cabbage tribe.

Pea Soup

One of my soups most appreciated by family and visitors alike is a green pea soup, a true 'throw-away' yet so delicious that one feels that it must be expensive. Some parts of it take so long to prepare, though, that I prepare it while I am watching the television.

When using peas for another dish set aside the pods and retain the onion-flavoured water in which they were cooked. The soup is made from the pods, but first of all their tough inner membranes have to be peeled away. It is this which takes the time. Start at the stem and pull. If you do it properly the whole of the papery inner skin should come away in one go. Practice makes perfect.

Boil the pods until tender. Flavour them with mint if you like. I then put pods and liquid in the electric blender and finally sieve them. This ensures that any little bits of tough tissue do not get into the soup. Taste and adjust seasoning and flavouring if necessary.

Serve the soup either piping hot or well chilled. To chilled soup I add chopped walnuts, radish, baby carrots, chervil, parsley, mint, very finely sliced spring onion, cream, yogurt, well-beaten egg and lemon juice. Sometimes I set dishes of these various extras on the table so that guests can help themselves as they do when eating gazpacho. Croûtons of fried bread, pieces of crispy bacon and mixed green herbs are good with hot soup. A dash of cream makes all the difference. Thin with stock to the required consistency before serving.

Peas with Fennel

Make a good bunch of the soft green leaves of fennel. Put it in boiling water, salted, with the peas and cook in the usual way. Drain the peas, add a little butter and just before serving sprinkle over them 1tbsp chopped fennel. This dish is splendid with scrambled egg.

Growing sugar peas

As time goes by I find that I grow less and less of the varieties that have to be shelled and more and more of the mangetout varieties, known also as sugar peas. Most seedsmen nowadays list these. They are a very economical crop; they are eaten whole, so there is no waste and little time involved in preparing them.

These peas should be gathered as soon as the tiny seeds are swelling

in their pods. You can easily see how they are progressing by lookin
at the pods against the light. It is important to gather before they gro
too large or the peas will be mealy and the pods tough.

Grow them in the same way as any other early peas. Sow in succes
sion; as soon as one row appears above ground, sow the next. Row
need not be long if you are a small family. Sugar peas do well and cro
early if they are grown under cloches. They vary in height accordin
to their variety. Sweet Green, a favourite of mine, is 3ft high. Dwarf d
Grace, which has very long pods, is 3–4ft, and Carouby de Maussane
the true, flat mangetout pea, is 5ft.

Cooking sugar peas

Preparation is simple; all you have to do is top and tail them. Use
small knife and begin at the tail (stem), end. You will find that as yo
pull the tail towards the top the string around the outside of the pe
comes away with it. Repeat the process at the top.

These peas are excellent as a first course. Cook them until tender
usually about 10–15min, and serve with butter.

If you reap a bumper harvest and do not wish to freeze the peas, the
will last for at least a week in plastic bags or boxes in the refrigerator
Those which mature from late (June), sowings seem to keep ever
longer. Do not top and tail them until you are ready to use them.

Growing petit pois

The most common variety of petit pois is Gullivert which grows to
height of 3ft. This can be sown from March to June. The plants carry
heavy crops, but of course you need more of them to fill the same dish
as English garden peas. Like all peas, petit pois are best cooked young.

Cooking petit pois

Peas French Style

1qt shelled peas	$\frac{1}{4}$lb butter
1 good hearty lettuce without outside leaves, finely shredded	2tsp salt
	4tsp sugar
12 very small onions	4tbsp water
1 small bunch parsley and chervil	

Put all of these in a pan and mix well. Cover. Bring to the boil, turn down the heat and simmer gently. When the peas are tender take out the herbs and serve. It usually takes about 15–20min.

Growing asparagus peas

Here's another plant for those who want to marry one part of the garden with another. This is a flowering annual which produces odd, almost rectangular-shaped pods, which really are asparagus flavoured.

It is forbiddingly named *Tetragonolobus purpureus*, synonym *Lotus tetra etc.* Its flowers are prettier than its name, deep red and very prolific. The plant itself is rather like clover.

The little plants make an attractive border to a bed or path, or alternatively they can be grown in groups among other annuals. They need to be spaced 6–12in apart to grow well. They naturally sprawl attractively, but if the plants are supported the pods will be easier to gather and will also keep cleaner. Apart from sticks, you can use a narrow piece of wire netting folded tent-wise. If this is placed over the plants they will grow up through it.

Sow the seed, individually if possible, in early April to the end of May.

Cooking asparagus peas

The important thing about asparagus peas is to pick them really young, not long after the flower has faded. If you fail to do this you will find that the peas are 'bony'. They are four-flanged and seem when old to have a stiffening in them to keep them in shape. If you grow only a few plants store each day's picking in plastic boxes or bags in the refrigerator until there is sufficient for a full dish. Cook them whole. No preparation is necessary.

Like all young vegetables the pods will need cooking only for a few minutes. I like to bring salted water to the boil, put in the pods, let it boil again, simmer for 5min and then turn it off. The pods can remain in this water for a few minutes longer while other preparations for the meal are going forward.

If you intend to serve them cold, give them the same accompaniments as asparagus. Save the water in which they have been boiled for a good, creamy, asparagus-type soup. Better still, purée some of the peas to go in it.

If you have a freezer

You may find it more convenient to do away with successional sowing and grow just one kind of pea and at one time only. I prefer to grow a succession of crops because I am not then overwhelmed with great quantities of peas to process at one time.

Blanch very young peas for 1min and leave headroom when they are packed. Blanch pods for 2min if you want to save them for soup. Alternatively blanch pods whole for 2min and separate later.

Top and tail the sugar peas and mangetout and blanch these for 2min. Allow headroom.

PEPPERS

Growing

This is an exotic vegetable-fruit which should be grown in much the same way as the tomato. Until now the great difference between the two has been that the capsicums have not been bred with northern climates in mind as has the tomato. The latter seems to improve each year. However, a new variety of pepper, Canape, grows well once planted outdoors, if placed in a warm, sunny, sheltered spot. The fruits of Canape are smaller than those of older varieties.

There is no problem if you have a sunny greenhouse. If you doubt whether you have a suitable site in the open garden, the plants can be grown in pots or other containers against a warm south wall.

In any case none must be put outside until early June and even then, should the early summer prove cool, the plants should be protected at night. A large plastic bag pulled over each one should do the trick. Be sure to remove it before the sun plays on the plants in the morning.

Sow the seeds, individually if possible, into small pots (peat pots save a lot of work later on) in a temperature not lower than 65° F, 18° C. Don't be despondent if the plants seem to lag, for they are usually slow at first. Water freely and once the plants are really growing well feed them as you would feed tomatoes and with the same kind of fertiliser. In bright sunny weather plants benefit from a light syringing. As in the case of tomatoes again, humidity aids pollination.

It is wise to tie each plant to a cane or some other stake. However, cultivation of the pepper is less demanding than that of the tomato. No trimming or training is necessary.

If you want red peppers let the fruits remain on the plant until they ripen. Cut fruit from the stems; if you try to pick them you may damage the plant.

Cooking (see also Red Cabbage)

Spanish Peppers (serves 4)

This is a good dish to serve with rice.

4 peppers (I like to use various
   coloured ones)
4tbsp olive oil
2 medium onions (tops as well
   if you have them)

2 cloves garlic
4 fairly large tomatoes
pepper and salt

Chop garlic finely, slice onions. Cut each pepper in half lengthwise, remove seeds and cut into thick strips. Heat the oil in a shallow, heavy pan and add garlic, onions and peppers. Skin and slice the tomatoes and set them aside. Fry the contents of the pan slowly. When they are almost cooked add the tomatoes. Stir them in well with a wooden spoon. Add the seasoning. Let all cook for a few minutes longer, that is until the tomatoes also are cooked.

PLUMS

Growing
On the whole plums grow into large trees. Even those sold as 'dwarf' or half-standards assume dimensions which are too great for the average garden. They need to be planted at least 12–15ft apart. Unfortunately they are not so amenable to training as are most other fruits. Fan-trained plants have proved to be the most satisfactory type but in my opinion these are best left to the skilled gardener since they need special pruning, even root pruning. However, choice plums can be grown this way against a house, wall or fence or even trained along boundary wires. There is an advantage, of course, in that these fan-trained trees can easily be protected against frosts and netted against birds. Plums are among the first fruit trees to flower, so they should only be planted where the site is known to be fairly frost free.

Another important point, and one which if not observed can result in poor cropping, is that some plums will set (form fruit) with their own pollen, but there are others that need cross pollinating. If you have an old tree in your garden which gives a poor performance it may be that it is not a self-fertile variety. If you are planting two or three plums include one which is known to be self-fertile. The fruit nurseryman will help you choose suitable varieties.

Plums do not like a very dry climate. They must be planted in a well-drained soil in which plenty of humus has been incorporated and which will continue to be mulched annually with the well-rotted manure or even peat. And as with all stone fruits there must be some lime present in the soil, either natural or applied. On the other hand, this is not to say that plums will do well on chalky soils or on thin soils below which chalk lies. Too much lime induces an iron deficiency in some plants, even in some which need lime. This can be rectified but may prove expensive. It is best if you intend growing plums to take out planting holes that are really much larger than necessary and to fill these with a soil rich in humus.

It helps to feed the trees annually once they have begun to crop well. As well as the annual mulch, in February, apply 1oz nitro-chalk and ½oz sulphate of potash per sq yd. If you have used peat instead of manure, double the amount of nitro-chalk.

Cooking

If you have inherited a plum tree which does not yield fruit of first quality, but is sound all the same, try pickling them.

Pickled Plums

4lb plums
2lb brown sugar
1pt spiced vinegar (this is made by boiling 2pt of malt vinegar with 2oz mixed pickling spice)

Remove the stalks from the plums and wash them. Prick them all over with a fork. This helps to keep them whole when they cook. Boil the vinegar and sugar together for 5min. While the liquid is still boiling put in the plums and simmer them for about 8–10min or until they are tender but not broken. Using a perforated spoon lift them into warm jars. Boil the vinegar again and pour it over the fruit. Cover the jars.

Plums into Prunes

If you are surrounded by plums, with no room in the freezer or no more jars for preserving them, you might like to dry some.

Choose good, unblemished, unsplit fruits. Find some shallow wooden boxes—clean seed-boxes are ideal for the purpose. If they have been used, scrub them well and line them with kitchen paper.

Put the plums in the box in tightly packed rows, stalks uppermost. Cover them with more kitchen paper. Place the boxes where they can dry—a cool oven perhaps—but the temperature should not rise higher than about 150° F, 65° C. If you use an airing cupboard, leave the door open a little. A friend of mine dries her plums by the glass in a green-house, and in hotter climates one can often see fruit, peppers and others, drying in the sun.

The plums will soon begin to shrink, so simply push them together a little more. When they look like prunes pack them into airtight storage jars or canisters and store in a dry place.

If you have a freezer
First wash, and then skin and halve the plums placing them cut-side downwards in a deep dish. When one layer has been made, sprinkle brown sugar over the plums and begin another layer. Continue until you have sufficient plums in sugared layers to meet your needs. Cover and let them stand for a few hours before serving them with cream.

For a special occasion pour a little brandy over them first and if you like contrasts of textures, add a few blanched almonds.

For freezing have ready plastic containers or whatever you normally use for storage and prepare the plums in these. Leave ½in headroom. Cover and freeze.

POPPIES

Growing

Some of the most attractive annual poppies are *Papaver somniferum* varieties. These are beautiful double flowers which are called by such names as 'Paeony flowered' or 'Carnation flowered'. The species is in my view also beautiful, being single with either dusky-rose or lavender-coloured petals. I grow the plants for flower arrangement, all parts being beautiful, not least the attractively shaped seed vessels which I used in both fresh and dried arrangements. When these are gathered and hung upside down to dry, the rich oily seeds soon cascade from them.

If you want these for cooking the best method of collecting them is to let a few pods grow really large and ripe. You can shake them gently and listen to the seeds rustling inside. Gather the seed stems, put a bag over their heads, turn them upside down and shake the seeds into the bag. Store in a stoppered jar or canister.

You can sow the seeds like other hardy annuals in September so that they will stand the winter and flower early, and you can also sow in March.

Cooking

I use the seed mainly when making bread. Rolls, painted over with milk or water just as they are almost finished and then sprinkled with seed and returned to the oven for a minute or two, are given a delicious flavour.

Taking a leaf from a Hungarian friend's cook book, poppy seeds can be mixed with cream and sugar, flavoured with orange or lemon peel and used as toppings or fillers for cakes and scones.

Poppy Seed Dressing

½ cup sugar
1tsp each salt, dry mustard,
   celery seed,* poppy seed

1tbsp very finely chopped onion
   and shallot
1 cup (½pt) olive oil
4tbsp vinegar or lemon juice

Mix the sugar, dry spices and onion together. Then add the olive oil, slowly beating well. You can use an electrix mixer for this. Add the vinegar or lemon juice.

This dressing is very good with any cold, cooked vegetable, especially all peas and beans.

If you wish to make it richer, begin with an egg yolk, mayonnaise fashion, add the mustard and salt, beat well with a wooden spoon for a minute or so before adding the oil drop by drop. You will then find that it thickens quickly. Continue beating. Once the mixture is thick, let the oil run in a thin stream. When all the oil is blended add the onion and shallot, then the vinegar or lemon juice and finally the seeds.

* Never use celery seed, nor any other seed for that matter, from a garden seed packet. Celery seed is almost always dressed with fungicides and most seeds receive some dressing or another to help them germinate better, grow more quickly or ward off pests and diseases.

POTATOES

Growing
Potatoes can play a double role, for besides helping to feed a family they also help to clean, and even cultivate, the soil.

I question the wisdom of putting down very large areas to this crop except for the reason expressed above, but I would certainly urge every vegetable grower to try just a row or two of some special potato, preferably an early variety, mainly for the unforgettable flavour and the sheer basic pleasure of digging the tubers. One can choose varieties like Jaune d'Hollande which taste delicious but which are not normally found on sale simply because they do not crop heavily enough to make them a commercial proposition.

Fortunately from Suttons at least one can still buy the Pink Fir Apple potato, also known as the Salad potato. This has pink, oddly shaped tubers, but delicious lemon-coloured waxy flesh which retains that wonderful new potato taste which seems even to be stronger when the potato is eaten cold.

Begin caring for potatoes as soon as they are bought, in January or February. Store them in a frost-free but airy place and take them from their bags. Stand them out on trays, the eye end uppermost so that the shoots can become influenced by the light and begin growing. This process is known as 'chitting'. Later, if you find that a potato has not developed its shoots, do not plant it.

Depending upon the weather and the condition of the soil (if this sticks to the soles of your shoes then it is too wet) you can begin planting early types outdoors in a sheltered place in early March, with main crop varieties in April. Spacing for earlies should be 1ft apart for tubers with rows 2½ft apart. Main crop potatoes need just a little more room in each direction.

Once the potatoes show through the ground the soil on each side of the plant should be drawn up to protect the shoots. This gives the effect of a ridged row. More earthing up will be necessary throughout the following weeks. This process serves to clear and cultivate the ground. You may need to do this several times, both to remove the little fuzz of annual weeds that is sure to appear on any fertile soil and to keep your growing tubers covered.

There are new ways of gardening now that are much easier and quicker than the old. For instance, if your plot is overgrown and weedy there is now no need to clear it by heavy and laborious digging before you can plant your tubers. You can use instead a chemical weedkiller which will safely do the job for you. One such preparation is called Weedol, and it is important that it is not confused with any other product with a similar name, for where Weedol leaves the soil clean, uncontaminated and healthy, some weedkillers render it unproductive and even poisoned.

When planting the potatoes use a garden line and, keeping the correct spacing, dig a hole with a trowel or spade for each tuber and then cover it again. You can use your Weedol before or after planting. It comes in the form of granules which must be thoroughly mixed with water and applied as a fine spray. The main virtue of Weedol is that although it kills all the green growth it touches, it does not affect woody stems such as trees and it becomes completely inactivated once it touches the soil. Some of the more persistent weeds such as couch grass, dandelions, docks and convolvulus may need several applications before they finally die.

When the potato shoots appear above the ground you can still spray any weeds that may have grown, but you will have to take the greatest care not to let any of the weedkiller drift on to the potato leaves. If this should happen then you must either wash it off with clean water immediately or tear off the sprayed leaf from the plant. At this stage you also have the alternative of hoeing away any young weeds that may appear, and perhaps this will be the safer activity as they will certainly be young and susceptible.

There is some evidence that land treated this way is more fertile than soil which has been first dug and cleaned and then planted. You can leave the debris of the dying weeds to be dragged under the soil by the worms, for the more of these there are the better your soil will become and decaying refuse or humus helps to increase the worm population. But if the untidy mess offends you, then by all means rake it off.

To earth up or ridge your potatoes simply hoe the soil between the rows and then pull the soil from one side of the row on to the row of plants nearest to it and the other half to the potatoes on the other side.

There is another and quite different method of growing potatoes, preferably on land which is already weed free. This makes use of strips of black polythene sheeting which inhibits the growth of weeds and saves all digging. Simply lay the potatoes on the ground in rows and at the proper intervals and cover them with the plastic sheeting. This must be weighted down against the wind and the easiest way to do this is to cover the edges with soil. When the potato shoots grow and begin to push against the plastic, cut little slits in it so that they can grow through, but so that little or no light can penetrate the sheeting. The new potatoes will grow on the ground surface and will not have to be dug. This means that you can lift the plastic, select a few of the largest specimens for immediate use and then cover the remainder for later.

Both the chemical weedkiller and the plastic sheeting will add to the overall cost of your potatoes, so if saving is your main objective and if you have time and energy to spare, the best method of growing them is the old one. This will present you with dividends at the end, for you will have cleaned and cultivated your ground and will be able to follow your potato crop with winter greens or salads.

Cooking

Potatoes can be made to play all kinds of roles in emergencies, even taking the place of pastry in a pie. If you grow your own you will find that some of them are unlike any you buy. These are the tiniest tubers which are usually among the mass when you lift a root. Wash them well, dry them and either fry them whole in a deep fat as you would chips, or have ready some very hot fat in a baking tin in a hot oven, and roast them. Twenty minutes or so should be long enough.

Baked potatoes in their jackets are best when they are well scrubbed, slit around the centre to break the skin, rubbed all over with a little olive oil or dripping and then lightly sprinkled with salt. Place them on the oven shelf and allow about 1hr at moderate heat. If you want to hurry them because the meat is ready and they are not, finish them off under the grill, turning them often so that the skin does not become charred.

Some potatoes are better than others for certain forms of cooking. Among the main crops the popular King Edward has a high quality, and although it is quite good for chips it is not as good as Desirée which is also a good all-rounder. Redskin, sometimes labelled King Edward in shops as several other red-skinned varieties are, is not at all good for chips but is a good, floury, mealy potato and good for mashing.

Party Potato Chips

Take fairly large potatoes and cut them in thin slices. Then take sweet or pastry cutters and cut out shapes. We used teddy bears, Scottie dogs, ducks and rabbits. The chips cook quickly because they are thin and they soon become nice and brown.

Potato Crisps

Children can also help you to make potato crisps. Give them the thinnest potatoes you can find (scrub them well first) and a potato peeler. Show them how to cut the slices across the potato with the peeler. As they are cut they should be laid on kitchen paper to dry in the air a little. You had better do the frying because they should be fried very quickly in deep fat. Drain on kitchen paper and serve.

Potato Creams, to Serve with a Boiled Fish Dish

3 cups mashed potatoes
½ cup whipping cream
salt, paprika, pinch cayenne

½ cup grated cheese
1tbsp chopped chervil

Whip cream and season with salt, paprika and pepper and blend it with the cheese and chervil. Place the mashed potatoes on an oven dish in a mound. Cover this with the cream mixture so that it is coated all over. Bake in a moderate oven at about 380° F, 190° C until all is lightly browned, about 20–30min.

Potato Puffs

This is a basic dish into which you can put all kinds of other foods, from mixed fresh herbs, chives, crisp bacon pieces or well chopped ham, chicken, tinned fish to grated cheese or whatever takes your fancy. Or they can be served perfectly plain. And if you care to leave out the seasoning you can add dried fruit and serve the puffs with sugar as a sweet.

¾ cup mashed potato
½ cup self-raising flour
good pinch salt

1 egg well beaten
2tbsp milk

Mix the flour and salt into the potato. Mix the milk with the egg and add to the potato mixture. Beat all well. Have ready a deep frying pan with hot oil. Drop small spoonfuls into the oil. Lift them out as they brown and drain them on kitchen paper. Keep the puffs warm and serve at once.

Potato Wine

This is a strong wine which can be used as an apéritif or a nightcap In the first case chill and serve with a little lemon zest.

5 large old potatoes
juice and rind of 2 lemons and
    1 orange
1tsp ground ginger

3½lb demerara sugar
yeast
4oz seedless raisins

Scrub the potatoes and cut them into large pieces, boil them in 1gal of water for about 15min. Strain while the potatoes are still firm. Boil the liquid again, this time with the rinds and the ginger for 10min. Mark level. Add more water if the level drops below the gallon mark. Have the sugar ready in a bucket. Pour the boiling liquid over it. Stir well. When lukewarm, add the fruit juices and the prepared yeast liquid. Cover and leave to ferment, stirring daily. When fermentation slows down pour all into a fermentation jar. Add raisins and insert airlock. Leave for at least 9 months, then rack off into bottles.

PUMPKINS

Growing
Just the same way as marrows.

Cooking
In any way recommended for marrow and squash, but don't forget that it makes delicious sweets. Remember those famous American pumpkin pies! For pumpkin jam follow the melon jam recipe.

The best way to de-pulp a pumpkin is to wipe it, cut it in half, de-seed, put it cut-side down on a baking dish and bake it at about 325° F, 165° C until tender.

Pumpkin Soup

1lb pumpkin	1pt water
3oz potatoes	1½oz rice
2oz onions	1tbsp butter
4 medium tomatoes	1tbsp cream

Peel and cut up all vegetables and put them in the water with the seasoning. Boil and simmer for ½hr. Add rice and simmer a little longer until this is tender, or if you like, use cooked rice. Serve with crisp toast spread with parsley butter.

Pumpkin Chiffon Pie

1 9in short-crust pie shell	½lb fine sugar
1¼ cups pumpkin pulp	½ cup (¼pt) milk
1tbsp gelatine	½tsp cinnamon
3 eggs	½tsp nutmeg
4tbsp cold water	pinch salt

Soak the gelatine in water. Divide eggs and beat the yolks to mix them, add to them half the sugar, pumpkin, milk and spices. Cook these together in a double saucepan or over hot water until the mixture thickens. Stir in the gelatine and water which should be well mixed. Continue to stir until this dissolves.

When cool and the mixture begins to set stir in rest of sugar, whip the egg whites with the pinch of salt and when these are stiff fold them into the mixture. Fill the pie shell. Put it in the refrigerator to chill thoroughly. Make the pie in the morning if you intend to serve it in the evening. To serve, decorate with whipped cream.

If you have a freezer
Cook the pumpkin and pack it in containers leaving a little headroom.

QUINCES

Growing

The common quince is *Cydonia oblonga*, syn *C. vulgaris*. This has white or pale pink blossom and apple- or pear-shaped fruits with a distinctive perfume and it crops fairly well.

What is often also called quince is the fruit of a variety of the so-called 'flowering quince', *Chaenomeles speciosa*, often called 'japonica'. These are beautiful plants flowering early and often completely colouring a wall against which they are trained. Not all produce fruits, and even those which do may produce only a few. If you have no more than one or two, make the most of your unsolicited gift and include the fruits in an apple pie when next you make one. The quinces will give it a delicious aroma.

Quinces also make excellent jelly.

Quince Jelly

Wash and quarter the fruit, no need to peel. Place in a pan and just cover it with water and cook gently until it is soft and pulpy. Turn it into a jelly bag and let it drip for about 24hr. Measure the juice and to each pint reserve 1lb preserving sugar. Warm the sugar in the oven while the juice is boiling. Add the one to the other. Bring back to the boil and continue to boil until the liquid will set, which should be in about 15min. Have warm jars ready. Pour into these and cover.

R

RADISHES

Growing

Few of the many radishes I grow are in their own rows, for I sow some seeds in almost every drill I draw for other vegetables. Radishes germinate and mature so much more quickly than the rest; they are always pulled by the time the other crop wants more room.

I draw the drill the proper depth for the main vegetable, and if this is deeper than needed for radish, ½in in their case, I cover the seed with a little moist peat or soil, sow the radish very thinly on this, cover them and firm down by lightly treading along the row. Otherwise I sow the main seed first and then go back along the row with the radish seed and cover the drill as usual.

The only seeds I don't mix with radishes are peas, in case the tiny tendrils begin to cling to the radish leaves.

Quick growth is essential for succulent roots of all kinds. For radish you need a moderately rich loam. I use a lot of peat, lining most drills and covering seeds with it before topping it with soil. Use it moist to help the seeds germinate more quickly.

Summer radishes can be sown as early as February if you have a warm, sheltered site, or you can sow them under cloches or in frames. Keep making fresh sowings. As soon as you see one crop showing above the soil put in another. Go on doing this until July and then switch to winter types. These are much larger, suitable for grating for winter salads. Sow China Rose in July and up until the end of August for lifting in November and storing in dry sand or peat. Black Spanish Radish, a long black root, can be sown in September to stand the winter and can be pulled as required.

There are several varieties of radish. My own favourite is French Breakfast, which is red with white tips. If you like playing around with salads this is the variety which opens up best and resembles a flower when you cut it down in petal sections from root towards tip. Soak the cut roots in water and they will open.

The 'gold' in new varieties of some vegetables such as beet and courgettes has spread also to radish. Yellow Gold has a milder, less radishy flavour.

Cooking

Every portion of a radish plant is edible. If by chance you have some which have gone to seed, slice the pods and use them in sandwiches.

Young, tender leaves can be used raw in salads or they can be cooked like spinach. I often cook them in a little stock, blend in the mixer and then use them to make a chilled soup. Always remove the stems before cooking large leaves as these can be tough and fibrous.

In summer I have radishes fit to pull every day. We like to nibble them before a meal as an appetiser. I also use them in the following ways: chopped and mixed with chopped herbs in soups either hot or chilled—put in at the last moment so that they remain crisp; to blend with the yolk of hard-boiled eggs and butter as a stuffing for the whites; mixed with chopped walnuts and stirred into yogurt, mayonnaise and cream cheese as a salad. Large ones are sliced and covered with French dressing; put into a white sauce, again at the last moment, then used to cover sliced tomatoes and cucumbers.

Cooked pink radishes are delicious, although they lose their bright colour. First blanch them for 5min in boiling salted water, then take them out and stew them in butter, a little white stock, gravy or cream. I don't peel young radishes, but the larger, older specimens have tough skins which should be removed for cooking.

RASPBERRIES

Growing

I grow one row of raspberries at the end of our kitchen garden cage. The row runs from north to south and thus receives the greatest possible amount of sun. I keep the row free of weeds by putting down a deep mulch of grass cuttings, usually as soon as we begin cutting the lawns in the spring. This also helps to keep the roots cool. Furthermore it inhibits the production of suckers which raspberries tend to throw up some distance away from each cane. Raspberry roots are very near to the surface so mine soon benefit from the moisture which is retained by this practice.

The canes should be planted singly and about 18in apart. As they grow they fill this space and become one continuous row. They are very simple to deal with. All you have to do is cut down to ground level the canes or stems which have borne fruit. Usually by the time you are ready to do this the new canes have appeared.

To secure the plants erect two or more strong posts from which wire can be strung in parallel rows. Tie the canes to the wires as they grow. If they become very tall, either cut the tips or bend them down and tie the tips to the top wire. It is said that one should reduce the number of canes at each plant or stool to three or four, but I must confess that I do not do this.

Each autumn I give the plants a deep mulch of manure. I do not fork it in, wishing to make sure that the roots near the surface are not harmed in any way.

Raspberries seem to be hungry plants. Mine grow quite well with the grass and manure mulching and the added benefit of wood ash from the house fires which are sometimes lit in winter, but you could apply sulphate of potash in the autumn at $\frac{3}{4}$oz per sq yd.

I have tried the autumn fruiting varieties, but these do not do well in our garden which attracts autumn mists. However, there are districts where these varieties do well. I find that the summer berries freeze so well that I do not really need to plan for a longer season.

Cooking
Loganberries can be used in the same way as raspberries in any recipe.

Raspberry Conserve

My objection to stewing raspberries, or most soft fruits come to that, is that the seeds become so hard that they spoil the texture of the flesh. This often applies when the fruits are made into jam. If you, too, feel this way, try this conserve recipe. You cannot keep it for as long as you would keep jam, but even so it will store for many weeks. When the raspberry season is past, you can use this conserve in many kinds of simple sweets—mixed in with whipped cream, for instance.

To each 1lb raspberries allow 1lb fine sugar. Put each separately into oven dishes, cover with foil and bake in a warm oven until they are really hot. Have the jars ready warming also. Remove the raspberries and bash-mash them with a wooden spoon so that there are no whole fruits. Add the hot sugar, stirring really well so that both are perfectly blended. Spoon into the hot jars and tie down.

Raspberry purées are worth making from the blemished fruits and these can then be stored or bottled. I like to serve a not very sweet purée with plain meringues. The sweetness of the one complements the sharpness of the other.

Raspberry Ice Cream

1 jar sweetened, bottled raspberries, or the equivalent in purée	1 heaped tbsp fine sugar, more if the raspberries have not been sweetened
½tsp powdered gelatine	1 gill top of the milk
½pt cream	

Sieve the raspberries and taste, adjusting sweetening if necessary. Make sure sugar is dissolved. Melt the gelatine in a little of the juice or purée made hot. Beat this into the rest until the gelatine is well dissolved.

Beat the cream with the sugar until it is thick. Thin the purée with the gill of milk if necessary. Gradually add this to the cream, beating slowly all the time. When all is well whipped and firm pour it into a tray or mould and put it in the freezing compartment of the refrigerator, in which case turn it back to front after an hour. Alternatively, put it in the deep freeze. It should be ready in two hours or so.

Pavlova Pie

This is adapted from an Australian recipe using raspberries instead of grenadines or passion fruit. (The latter are not the orange fruits our passion fruit vines produce, which unfortunately, cannot be cooked or eaten.)

First make a meringue pie shell. I use the electric mixer for this in the first stages. You will need:

3 egg whites	1tsp vinegar
good pinch of salt	1tsp water
1tsp vanilla essence, not	1 cup fine sugar
necessary if you use vanilla	½tsp baking powder
sugar	

Invert a large cake tin and grease the base. Alternatively use a large sponge or flan tin with a removable base and lightly oil that. Place a circle of greaseproof paper on the tin and brush this lightly with oil. You will then find it easy to remove the pie shell when it is baked.

Put the egg whites, salt, vinegar, water and vanilla together into the electric mixing bowl and mix until stiff. If you don't use a mixer, beat the egg whites first, then add the mixed liquids a little at a time. Mix the baking powder well with the last spoonful of sugar.

Keep on beating while the sugar is added gradually. I prefer to do this by hand. Beat until the meringue is stiff and will remain in peaks when lifted with a spoon. Empty the mixture on to the greased paper in such a way that you make a circle about 1in thick at the centre with a raised edge and within the circumference of the paper circle. Bake it at 275° F, 135° C, for an hour or longer if the meringue is not dry enough. You should be able to lift it from the paper. Let it cool. Carefully remove the paper as you slip the pie on to a plate. Just before serving pile on the fruit and top with whipped cream.

RHUBARB

Growing
Find a corner somewhere where this handsome plant can luxuriate, but don't hide it away! Plant it near the house for easy access and so that you can enjoy the sight of it.

Give it deep, rich soil and a sunny, open position. Plant lifted crowns and divide old ones in November, February or March or sow seeds in the open ground in March and April. Plant canister-grown rhubarb any time.

Be patient and don't pull any stems the first year and you will have rhubarb for ever. Cut off the flower stems as soon as they appear. Top dress the plants with manure or home-made compost in spring and autumn.

Force it early in the year either by covering the plant with a large pot, tub or deep box to shut out all daylight, or by using a cloche covered with black plastic. Cover any of these with *fresh* stable manure or fallen leaves to give additional warmth.

If you have plants to spare you can force them this way. You need a large black polythene bag or sack. Place a 2–3in layer of moist peat on the bottom. Put a crown of rhubarb on this. Surround it with more moist peat and take this up as far as the top of the root to the crown. Close the bag tightly. Stand it indoors in a warm place. Inspect it after 2–3 weeks to gauge the rate of growth but don't leave the bag open for more than a minute or two unless you pull some stalks. Re-tie and wait for more.

Roots for forcing this way should be lifted in November onwards and left on the ground exposed to the frost for a few days.

Cooking

Use rhubarb in pies, puddings, tarts, conserves, jams, pickles, wines, sorbets, salads. *Never* eat the leaves.

Try unskinned rhubarb cut into 1in lengths, sweetened with honey instead of sugar and very slowly baked in a covered casserole.

Serve rhubarb at breakfast instead of grapefruit. It is delicious with all kinds of cereals. For mixed vegetable salads, slice the raw, un-skinned stems wafer thin and use French dressing.

Use rhubarb to spin out other fruits in jams and pies.

Rhubarb and Raspberry Jam

4lb rhubarb, finely sliced   2½lb sugar
2lb raspberries

Put the rhubarb in a bowl, sprinkle the sugar over it, cover and leave for 12hr at least. Stir in the raspberries. Tip all into a preserving pan, bring slowly to the boil and continue boiling until the liquid thickens and will set. Pour into hot jars.

Rhubarb Wine

5lb rhubarb   thinly peeled rind and juice of
1gal water   1 lemon
3½lb sugar   ½lb raisins, chopped
     sherry yeast

Clean the stalks but do not peel. Slice thinly. Pour the cold water over the rhubarb and then allow it to stand for 5 days stirring daily. Strain and squeeze the pulp as dry as possible. Add the sugar, the chopped raisins, the thin lemon peel and its juice to the liquid. Put all in a pan and heat gently stirring all the time until the liquid is warm but not hot. Cool to luke warm and add the activated yeast. Cover and stand in a warm place for 24hr. Pour into the jar and insert an airlock. Bottle when ready.

If you have a freezer

Peel and/or wash well and cut into convenient lengths. Pack raw or blanch for 1min. Purée or strained juice can be frozen. Leave a little head space for all.

ROSEMARY

Growing

Rosemary is an attractive shrub and quite beautiful when covered with flowers in spring; it is a herb which I use frequently for cooking.

It will grow in any ordinary soil, but this should be well drained which may explain why it grows well as a contained plant. Rosemary likes a dry and sunny situation. It grows wild in southern Europe, which explains why in other countries it does best where it can be given shelter. It looks attractive when trained to cover walls and it will make a good hedge for sheltered places and gardens.

The plant is easily propagated by cuttings of half-ripened shoots which can be taken in late spring and summer. This is a pleasant plant to pass on, most people are delighted with it as a gift. It can be placed in empty places about the garden and even looks well planted among the paving on a terrace or patio.

Cooking (see Herbs)
If you have always reserved rosemary for lamb or veal, try it with some strong oily fish, for example, mackerel, tunny or herrings. Chop it finely and use it discreetly, because a few leaves can contribute a good deal of flavour. Sprinkle a little over the fish before grilling or frying them.

You can flavour sugar with rosemary, in the same way as you flavour it with vanilla. To do this reserve a glass jar for 1lb fine sugar. Have ready washed and dried about half a dozen good tips of rosemary. Place these in the jar and pour the sugar over them. Let it stand for several days, until when you remove the lid you can smell the herb. This sugar can then be used to flavour milk for desserts, milk puddings of all kinds, egg custards and junkets.

Roast Lamb's Liver and Rosemary

1lb liver in one piece	1 large onion finely chopped
2oz chopped bacon	1tsp chopped rosemary
6 thin rashers, smoothed with	1 cup breadcrumbs
palette knife to make wider	1 beaten egg

Slice a cut in the centre of the liver to make a pocket. Mix the chopped bacon, onion, rosemary and breadcrumbs together and bind with the egg. Stuff the liver pocket with this. Tie string around the liver piece in two places to close the pocket and hold it all in shape. Place it in an oven dish and cover it with the bacon rashers. Bake at 350° F, 180° C for 30min. Place on serving dish and keep warm while you make a brown gravy with the fat in the dish. Serve with redcurrant jelly.

ROSES

Growing

I won't go into any details of rose cultivation, which can either be nothing—just plant the bush and hope—or which could fill a book. Suffice it to say, grow at least one rose, and if you have a large garden, grow a large number. If you have a garden large enough to have to think of ways of filling space, grow species or shrub roses, and especially those which produce very large hips.

The rose is wholesome. You can eat flowers, fruit and even leaves if you so wish.

Cooking rose petals

Choose large petals. Wash them lightly and let them dry on kitchen paper. Dip each petal first in brandy and then in a light batter. Fry in deep fat. Serve them dusted with fine sugar.

Candied Rose Petals: Method 1

Do not use petals that have dropped, for these are already fading and dying. Instead, pluck the rose petals from a newly opened flower early in the morning while they are still moist with dew, taking care not to crack or bruise them. Wash them if you feel this is necessary and spread them out to dry on a piece of absorbent kitchen paper or a cloth. They must be completely dry before being candied.

Take the white of one egg, add ½tspn water and a pinch of salt and beat together until the white is quite stiff. This is for the coating. Have ready a shallow bowl containing a thin layer of sugar, or a sugar shaker. Dip the petals in the egg white and then cover them with sugar until they are heavily coated. Place them on wax paper to dry thoroughly. These can be eaten immediately as sweetmeats or used to decorate cakes and other confections, or they will store. Keep them crisp by laying them between greaseproof paper in a covered jar.

This method can be used to candy other flowers and mint leaves, too.

Candied Rose Petals: Method 2

Make a syrup from 1½lb sugar and 1pt water.

Boil the petals in it six times for about 5min each time, allowing them to cool completely between each boiling. After the sixth boiling the petals should be transparent. Remove them and spread on kitchen paper. Sprinkle with fine sugar. To store, line a box with waxed paper, fold this over the crystallised petals so that they are completely surrounded, and make sure that the box is airtight.

Cooking rose hips

Many roses, even the modern hybrids as well as the species, produce large, luscious-looking fruits. Unfortunately one cannot simply pick these from the bush and nibble them, at least not without suffering from a ticklish throat for hours afterwards, for the seeds in the centre of the hips are coated with fine, tough and highly irritating hairs. However, the flesh is good to eat, and rich in vitamin C.

You can use these fruits in ways that you use many other fruits. I once knew an old cook who made a speciality of rose-hip tart, and extremely good it was too. The hips can be dried and stored and used in winter and early spring, when other fruits are scarce and expensive. Soak before use. Those gathered before frosts are sweeter than those picked later. Jam made earlier may need lemon juice to help it set.

Obviously the larger the hips the easier they are to prepare. First slit them open and remove all the seeds and small hairs. This is a fiddly job and one best done while you are looking at television with one eye or listening to music or the radio.

Rose-hip Sweet

½pt prepared rose hips	2tbsp cornflour
2pt water	½pt cream
4oz sugar	kirsch (optional)

Wash the rose hips well so that there are no hairs left in them. Put them in a heavy pan with the water. Bring slowly to the boil and then let simmer until the hips are soft and the water reduced. Stir from time to time. Either put in a blender or through a sieve. Boil the liquid with the sugar until it has dissolved. Skim the surface if this is necessary. Mix the cornflour with a little cold water and stir in and continue to stir until the liquid thickens. Allow to cool. Whip the cream until it is getting thick and then add it to the mixture. At this point you can add a little kirsch for flavouring. Pour into individual glasses.

Rose-hip Wine

4lb rose hips (best gathered
    after frost)
3lb sugar

peel and juice of 1 lemon
sherry yeast
1gal boiling water

Wash the fruits and either mince or chop them. Put them in a bucket
with the thin lemon peel, its juice and the sugar. Pour the boiling water
over all and stir well. Add the activated yeast when the liquor is lukewarm. Cover and leave for 10 days, stirring daily. Strain into jar, insert
airlock. Bottle when fermentation ceases.

S

SAGE

Growing (see Herbs)

There are several sages, all of them handsome plants and some, like the variety with multi-coloured leaves, really beautiful. If you have no special herb border, these are plants which, as evergreen shrubs, can grace any part of your garden. The narrow-leaved grey sage is *Salvia officinalis* and this has a variety with slightly wider leaves and violet colouring called *S. o.* var *purpurea*. There are also the golden sage with yellow variegated leaves and the multi-coloured sage already mentioned. The leaves from any of these can be used in cooking.

These are plants which like plenty of sun and light, rich, dry soil. You can raise them very easily from seed. As I write I have a little tray on the window-sill near me which was sown just over a fortnight ago and which already contains germinating seedlings. These will be potted into individual pots when they are larger and planted out in May or June. Sage grows easily from cuttings which are usually taken in April and put in a cold frame or under cloches. I manage to grow cuttings well at almost any time by putting them into individual pots and growing them indoors on a window-sill, not a sunny one.

It is important to keep the plants well picked, otherwise they become leggy and ungainly.

Cooking

Buckinghamshire Dumpling

1lb self-raising flour	2tsp chopped fresh sage
8oz suet	seasoning
½lb fat bacon or pork, chopped	milk
½lb pork liver, chopped	

Mix all together and add milk to make a stiff dough. Place in a greased basin. Cover first with greaseproof paper and then foil (each with a pleat at centre to allow for rising). Place in a large saucepan with hot water reaching at least halfway up the side of the basin. Bring to the boil and simmer for 2½hr. Serve with hot tomato sauce and spinach.

SALSIFY

Growing

This plant, *Tragopogon porrifolius*, produces delicious roots which can be eaten from mid-October and all through the winter until spring. It also produces shoots or chards in spring.

You need rich soil and a sunny, open site.

Sow the seeds in groups of three, 9in apart, in ½in deep drills in early April. Thin later to single plants. As they grow nip off the flower heads. Lift the roots in November and, after twisting off the leaf portion, store in layers in dry sand or peat until required. Leave some roots in the ground to provide chards in early spring.

Grow *Scorzonera hispanica*, or black salsify, in exactly the same way.

Cooking

The roots of both ordinary and black salsify are cooked in the same way and used in many fine dishes. The first has white-skinned roots and the second black, which are white when peeled.

The shoots can be cooked in the same way as the roots or eaten raw in salads.

Scrape or peel the roots and cut them into sections about 3in long. To prevent them becoming discoloured, put them into water to which a little lemon juice or vinegar has been added. They are best cooked in a court bouillon. Prepare this as follows:

Chop enough onion and carrot to give you a tablespoon of each. Finely chop 1 clove of garlic. Cook these three in 1oz butter or olive oil until they are soft but not browned. Stir in 1tbsp flour, add enough boiling water to cover the roots and stir until all is blended and smooth. Add a little lemon juice and seasoning.

Put in the roots, cover and cook slowly over a low heat for 2hr. To serve, take them from the court bouillon, put them in a hot dish and cover with butter or cream and chopped parsley.

You can also cover the cooked roots with French dressing when they have cooled and serve as a salad.

Another dish is to boil salsify in salted water with a little lemon juice. When the roots are tender, lay them in a buttered baking dish and sprinkle with salt, brown sugar, nutmeg and paprika. Dot them with butter. Pour single cream over them until the base of the dish is well covered. Bake in a hot oven, 400° F, 205° C, until the top is nicely browned.

SAVORY

Growing (see Herbs)

One of the most useful herbs is winter savory, *Satureia montana*, useful mainly because it is so hardy—you can even pick it in the snow. It is short, stocky and shrubby, nothing much to look at but it makes a good container plant.

So far as flavour goes, it is inferior to summer savory, *Satureia hortensis*, an annual and really very fragrant. Sow seeds for this in spring, where the plants are to be grown or raise the seedlings indoors and plant them out later.

Winter savory is best bought as a plant. It grows quite well from cuttings.

Both kinds will grow in ordinary soil and they both like plenty of sun.

Cooking

Savory is *the* herb for pork dishes, for veal and for duck. Like basil, it is also known as the 'bean herb'. Fresh sprigs should be boiled with young broad beans and with shelled green beans or flageolets. It suits any of the bean tribe, whether fresh or dried. Put a little into baked beans.

SHALLOTS

Growing

Plant shallots in rows across the vegetable garden, down the side of a sunny path, or here and there in odd patches, for these are the easiest vegetables to grow and among the most important. They are not raised from packeted seed but from individual bulbs known as 'seed'. Plant them 6in apart in rows 12in apart. You can plant them really early in the year. Country people use to advise planting them on the shortest day and taking them up on the longest. I usually plant mine in March.

Make a small depression in the soil with a trowel, plant the bulb and cover almost to the top. If you just press the bulb into the soil surface worms will move the shallots out of place.

The bulbs soon grow and later on divide into several other bulbs until you have a good cluster. You should wait until the leaves completely fade away before you lift them. Let the shallots become quite dry outside and then hang them in net bags to store.

There are two kinds of shallots: those with yellow and those with red skins. The first are not so strong, but they keep better during the winter.

After I have lifted mine I lay them on a piece of plastic under a cloche with open sides until the skins are dry and papery.

Cooking

Use shallots with onions to give a special tang to savoury dishes. Use the green tops as you would chives, that is, cut the leaves for garnishing and for salads and sauces.

Make shallot butter for hors d'oeuvres and sandwiches or party snacks.

Bring 3oz shallots to the boil. Remove, cool under cold water and drain. Pound to a pulp and add an equal amount of butter. Blend or mix well. Use this for spreading on toast, bread or biscuits. Add chopped parsley and use for topping chops, steaks and other grills.

Do not cook shallots when you pickle them.

Pickled Shallots

I like these to remain crisp, so I boil the spices in the vinegar and allow this to cool thoroughly before pouring it over the shallots.

1qt shallots	$\frac{1}{4}$oz cloves
1$\frac{1}{2}$oz salt	$\frac{1}{4}$oz peppercorns
1qt vinegar	2oz sugar
$\frac{1}{2}$oz pickling spice	2 bay leaves

Peel the shallots, sprinkle them with the salt and let them stand all night. Wash them to remove the salt, drain and dry them well.

Pack them into jars, leaving enough headroom for the vinegar to cover them completely. Tap the jars from time to time as you fill them and the shallots will settle and make more room for others. Tie down or cover securely. They will be ready for eating in 2–3 months.

Make a special white sauce this way. Take 1tbsp of chopped onion, half as much of chopped shallot and 1 chopped clove of garlic. Gently melt them in 1tbsp butter. When all are transparent but not brown, stir in 1tbsp flour. Take off the heat and blend. Return to the heat, add $\frac{1}{2}$pt milk, stirring all the time.

You can use this as a base for all kinds of other dishes. For instance add a small tin of shrimps and pour it over hard-boiled eggs.

This sauce is also the basis of a soup. Merely add vegetable water or stock, a little cream and some chopped green herbs.

SORREL

Growing

A member of the dock family, sorrel is often included in the lists of savoury herbs, but since it is not used primarily for flavouring but more usually as a distinctive dish, it really does not belong in this category. Possibly the confusion arose because of the slackness of our vocabulary. Sorrel is a 'pot herb'. The true meaning of this term applies to such plants as are used to make certain soups, such as orach, spinach, sorrel, purslane, seakale and lettuce. To make matters more confusing, the term 'pot herbs' is often applied by some people to certain roots used in stews, such as carrots, turnips, parsnips, celery and swedes. These also are used in soups, but the results differ considerably.

I grow only two roots of sorrel and I find that these are sufficient for my needs. They are perennials and once planted they seem to go on for years. The soil should be rich and moist but not in the shade. The plants need watering well in hot, dry weather. Plants can normally be bought at any good garden centre where herbs are sold and so can be planted from their pots at any time. Otherwise, lift the plants from the ground in March.

It is important to keep the leaves picked frequently; they are at their best when young. Watch for slugs and snails around the plants. Cut off flower stems before they can mature.

Cooking

I use sorrel in various ways—by adding very young leaves to green salads when salad vegetables are scarce; in soup; cooked with peas and potatoes; or made into sauces for fish. I particularly like it in a green sauce, served with boiled ham.

To make this, first wash the sorrel well. Always put it to soak in a little salted water first in case it has been visited by garden fauna, tiny slugs in particular. Shred it fairly coarsely and put it into a pan with only enough water to cover the base of the pan, and a little salt. Cover the pan and bring it to the boil slowly. When it has boiled, turn the sorrel so that the top layer goes to the bottom. Cover it again and let it simmer 3–5min longer. Blend or sieve it. Mix the purée with half its own bulk of cream. Add seasoning. Serve hot.

It is worth noting that you can make a purée of sorrel and keep it in the refrigerator for several days. Follow the directions just given, but after sieving or blending, mix the purée with half its own bulk of melted butter. Put it in a covered jar and store.

Sorrel Soup

½lb sorrel
2oz butter
2 medium-sized onions, finely chopped
3 medium-sized potatoes, finely chopped
salt, pepper
3pt white stock

Melt the butter but do not let it brown. Add the onions and potatoes and seasoning. Cover the pan and let the contents simmer for 20min. Add the stock and sorrel. Bring all to the boil, cover and simmer for

5min. Put the soup in the blender or through a sieve. Reheat and serve with cream and croutons.

SPINACH

Growing

There are three types of leaf spinach other than the leaf or spinach beet I have already described. These are Long Standing Round or Summer, Long Standing Prickly or Winter (round and prickly refer to the seeds and not the leaves), and New Zealand, which is really a different plant altogether. The latter is useful because it does well on dry soils and in hot summers, but even so the very hard-coated seeds should be soaked in water for a few hours before they are sown.

If you have a sheltered garden you can make the first sowing of summer spinach at the end of February or the beginning of March, otherwise wait until the end of March or the beginning of April depending on the season. Continue sowing every 3 weeks until August if you want a good supply and then switch to the winter type.

Sow the seed about 1in deep and thin the plants to 9–12in apart.

Cooking

Leaf Spinach (serves 4)

1lb spinach	$\frac{1}{4}$ cup water
3tbsp olive oil or melted butter	$\frac{1}{2}$tsp salt

Wash the spinach well, removing any very thick stems. Place it in a pan with the melted, not hot, fat and water. Sprinkle with the salt. The pan will probably be very full, but merely press the spinach down then put the lid on. After 3–4min take a fork and turn the mass of leaves so that the top is at the bottom. Recover and let it finish cooking. It should take 5–10min over a fairly good heat. Drain and chop finely.

A green soup, similar to sorrel soup (page 155) can also be made from spinach, or even young nettles.

Spinach Pancakes

For these you need first to blanch some spinach, although if you have some left over this also may be used.

To blanch, simply parboil the spinach in plenty of boiling water for 2–3min, then cool it under running water and drain well. Put it into a sieve and press it down to expel as much water as possible. Chop it very finely.

Make the pancake batter in the usual way and use equal parts of spinach and batter. Season with salt, pepper and nutmeg. Mix well. It helps to use the electric mixer for this. Make the pancakes in the same way as if they were plain. Roll or fold into four and serve with melted butter and grated Parmesan cheese.

You can also lay these pancakes in an oven dish and cover them with a cheese sauce and bake or grill them.

If you have a freezer
You can freeze these pancakes.

To freeze spinach remove the stems, blanch for 2min. Allow a little headroom.

SQUASH

Growing

There are many varieties of squash and you can find seed of most of them in any good catalogue. They have lovely names like Banana, Crook Neck, Butternut, Gem, Hubbard, Royal Acorn and Table Queen. New varieties are also constantly being introduced.

They are best described as ornamental marrows, and indeed one firm at least is listing the names above under the heading Vegetable Marrows, possibly because squash themselves are so little known in Britain. They come in all shapes, sizes and hues. On the whole their flesh is drier and has more flavour than that of the large vegetable marrow.

Squashes are divided into summer and winter kinds. The latter are usually left on the plant to ripen thoroughly until the skins are almost wood-hard. They can then be stored and used throughout the winter until spring. This treatment can be applied to all kinds, but as a rule the summer squashes and some marrows such as courgettes are eaten young.

Grow them in the same way as recommended for marrows.

Cooking

In any way recommended for marrows and pumpkins. Most of these vegetables, when ripe, can be used like pumpkins in pies as a sweet. The flesh may be sweetened and served like stewed fruit, for after all these are near relatives of the melon. They make good jams and preserves (follow recipe for marrow jam) and pickles.

For an easy dishful of vegetables, try vegetable spaghetti. The mature fruits should be boiled unpeeled for about 20min and then cut open, but not seeded this time. The spaghetti-like inside is scooped out, seasoned and served with butter or a meat or tomato sauce.

Avocadella, or the Argentine marrow, a compact bush type like the courgette, has small avocado-like fruits which can also be served cold, after cooking, halved and filled or topped with some savoury such as shrimps. This variety can be eaten young or ripened and stored. Cook unpeeled.

Winter Squash Baked

Take a 3–4lb squash and wipe or scrub it. Bake it in a moderate oven until it can be pierced with a cocktail stick or wooden skewer. Remove and cut in half. Scoop out seeds and then take out and mash the pulp. To each cup of pulp add 1tbsp butter, 1tsp brown sugar, ¼tsp salt and a good pinch of ginger. Mix well. Add cream if desired.

You can use small summer squash as dishes, filled with good things to serve as a first course. Allow one squash per person. First steam the squash over boiling water until tender. Cut a slice off the stem and scoop out the seeds. Fill the cases with such things as chopped mushrooms with crisp bacon, shrimps in cream and a touch of curry, minced meat and well-seasoned tomatoes. Place the filled squash in a well-buttered oven dish. Bake until all are nice and hot, usually taking about 10min at 400° F, 205° C.

Squash Soup

1 cup cooked squash	1 saltspoon celery seed
1 small onion	salt, pepper, paprika
2tbsp butter	chopped chervil (optional)
2tbsp flour	cream (optional)
1qt milk	

Chop the onion and melt in the butter. Add the flour, blend, pour on the milk and stir until it thickens. Add the squash, seasoning and celery seeds. To serve add a little cream and the chervil.

Gem Squash Filled with Tunny, Tinned Shrimps or Salmon (serves 6)

3 squash, evenly sliced	black pepper
3 egg yolks	1tsp chopped fresh chervil
8oz tin of fish	1tsp lemon juice
2tbsp grated Parmesan cheese	nutmeg

Cut the squash around the centres, like grapefruit. Scoop out the flesh, keeping the skins intact. Discard any hard seeds. Mix the flesh with the egg yolks. Mix the tinned fish into a paste, beating skin, bones and liquor all together. Blend this in with the squash and egg mixture. Add the pepper, chervil, lemon juice and 1tbsp Parmesan. Blend well.

Divide this filling into six and stuff each half. Sprinkle a little more cheese and nutmeg on the top and place in a covered oven dish. Serve hot with a tomato sauce.

If you have a freezer
Cook, cool and pack, leaving a little headroom.

STRAWBERRIES

Growing
I grow old, new and alpine strawberries. The old ones, Royal Sovereign, are grown on the 3 year system. I have three rows, 1 year, 2 years and 3 years old. The 3 year-old plants are always thrown away after fruiting and a new row is made from rooted runners taken from the youngest row. This is a good, tidy system. I try to keep the rows far enough apart so that I can plant a row of early lettuce between them. Then when I cover the plants with cloches in February (this helps them to fruit early) the lettuces also benefit from the protection given.

Elsewhere I have a row of perpetual or remontant strawberry Gento. Modern strawberries have really changed the gardener's scene! Gento is a welcome variety for new gardeners because it will fruit the same year in which it is planted. Where people have plenty of strawberry plants they sometimes pick off strawberry flowers formed early in the year, say up until mid-June, to give the plants strength for a good autumn crop.

It is my experience that if the plants are well fed and mulched (I use manure in winter, grass mowings in summer) they just go on and on fruiting. There are always so many green fruits when the autumn begins that I have to cover them with cloches. One can expect to go on picking the fruits well into November. I grow these on a raised bed at the side of a trodden path where they face west and the soil is warm and well drained.

Growing alpine strawberries
These make an attractive edging to a border along a path. I grow a row down the shadiest side of the trodden path through my vegetable patch. Here the other crops growing at right angles to them give them essential shade.

160

Baron Solemacher has a real wild-strawberry flavour. Alexandria has larger fruits and Alpine Yellow is really delicious. It looks good mixed with the red ones.

If one of your plants produces a larger berry than the others, select it and keep dividing it until you have your own special strain.

You can raise alpines from seed, and once you have good 2-year-old plants divide alternate plants each year to keep them prolific.

Seeds can be sown, just covered, in boxes under glass any time from January to May. Prick them off when they are large enough to handle and when they are well grown plant them out 9–12in apart.

Give the plants a rich soil and partial shade. If you have to grow them in full sun, keep them well mulched and well watered in dry weather. I give mine really deep mulches of both moist peat and fresh lawn mowings, using the latter to cover the peat. Cover with cloches in autumn to prolong their season. Manure them well in winter.

Cooking alpine strawberries

Don't cook alpine strawberries. These delicious little fruits, served raw but made into dishes, are my mainstay for winter entertaining. 'Ambrosial' commented one guest, yet what she had enjoyed was merely cream, whipped with vanilla-flavoured icing sugar and kirsch into which a cup of frozen alpines had been stirred.

If you have a freezer

Alpine strawberries freeze well and thaw out much more like freshly picked fruits than do the larger kinds. The important thing is to gather them only when they are fully ripe, and this goes for all occasions and not just when you intend freezing them. You can tell because the red fruit *shines*. If you gather only a few one day, put these in a covered plastic box in the refrigerator until you have gathered more. Don't take them out of the freezer too early and let them thaw out still covered—they keep firmer this way.

SWEDES

Growing

Sow these in May or June in drills ¾in deep and thin out to 9–12in apart. Lift as required.

Cooking

In the same way as recommended for turnips. If you find them too moist after cooking you can thicken them and make them easier to serve by blending them with a little mashed potato.

Swede Soufflé

4tbsp cooked swede purée, well drained
2oz butter
2oz flour
1 gill cream or top of milk

1tbsp chopped walnuts (optional)
salt, black pepper
2 eggs

Melt butter, stir in and blend flour, add cream and stir until smooth. Remove from heat and add swede and nuts. Taste and season, using plenty of freshly ground black pepper. Add egg yolks, unbeaten, and blend. Whip the egg whites with a pinch of salt until stiff. Fold in lightly. Divide into individual soufflé dishes, well buttered. Bake at 375° F, 190° C for about 10–15min.

An attractive-looking dish can be made by blending cooked swedes with cooked peas and sprinkling with freshly chopped parsley. A little cream added to this lifts it to a special place.

SWEET CORN

Growing

Modern hybrids mature much earlier than the old ones did. One of the recent introductions, an All-American Selections Winner of 1971 called Extra Early Sweet, produces cobs 3 months after sowing. Moreover it tolerates cold summers and cool, damp nights, and will continue cropping until the early frosts.

It also claims another quality. Whereas most sweet corn loses its flavour once it is harvested, this variety is said to be four times as sweet after 48hr.

Either sow outdoors under cloches in April or May where the plants are to mature, or singly in small pots, from March to May in a warm greenhouse, in a warmed frame or on a warm window-sill.

Corn is best grown in blocks. Single rows become wind-buffered and are not so easily naturally pollinated as those which grow near each other on all sides. In my own garden I alternate courgette plants with yard-square blocks of corn planted or sown 9in apart. The corn grows straight and high while the courgettes spread on the ground. One crop makes way for the other. By growing them this way the same row of cloches does for both in the early days.

If you start the corn in pots, do not let the roots become pot-bound. Move them on to larger pots as soon as necessary.

Cooking
Sweet corn is often cooked for too long and this toughens it. 8–10min is nearly always enough. Serve immediately with butter and salt and pepper. A cocktail stick pushed into each end makes a cob easier to hold if you have no special corn holders.

Baked Corn and Lettuce

2 cups (1pt) corn—shave it from
   the cobs with a sharp knife
$\frac{3}{4}$ cup milk
2 eggs

$\frac{1}{4}$ cup finely shredded lettuce
$\frac{1}{2}$tsp salt
$\frac{1}{2}$ cup white breadcrumbs
2tbsp butter

Combine the milk with the eggs, corn, lettuce and salt. Have ready a well-buttered baking dish. Place half this mixture in the dish, cover with half the breadcrumbs and dot with half the butter. Spread the other layer and cover in the same way. Pour the milk over it. Bake at 325°F, 165°C for 30–40min.

Sweet Corn Fritters (serves 4)

These seem almost obligatory for certain dishes—fried chicken for instance—but unless they are made well they can be so soggy and heavy. Try this recipe. It is a good one for many fritters, including flower and leaf fritters.

1 egg white
$\frac{1}{2}$tsp salt
$\frac{1}{2}$tsp baking powder

1 heaped tbsp flour
$\frac{1}{2}$ cup ($\frac{1}{4}$pt) corn, scraped from
   the cob

Beat the egg, salt and baking powder together until stiff (you can use an electric mixer for this quite satisfactorily). Fold the flour into the mixture, but do not beat or whip. Add the corn. Fold until all is well mixed. Deep fry by dropping spoonfuls into the fat. Fry until golden brown. Drain well on kitchen paper.

If you have a freezer

Choose only really young corn cobs, for freezing has a toughening effect. Blanch for 4min and drain on kitchen paper. Wrap each cob in freezer paper and freeze individually.

Cream corn or scraped corn can be frozen and will keep well.

T

TARRAGON

Growing (see Herbs)

There are two varieties of tarragon, *Artemisia dracunculus*. The best of these is considered to be the French tarragon. This has dark-green smooth leaves. The other variety is Russian tarragon, with leaves less smooth and a taste not quite so sharply pungent.

Tarragon is a perennial but it sometimes fails to live through the winter if the weather is severe. It should therefore be given some protection. It grows best in sunny borders and in warm, dry soils. It is a good container plant. I have a plant in a tub together with other herbs and this produces shoots in late winter and early spring some weeks ahead of the plants in the open herb border.

It is best to buy plants to make sure of getting a good strain. They can be propagated by pulling the underground runners away from the main plant. Do this in April. Replant annually for best results.

Plants can be lifted and planted in boxes or pots for forcing throughout the winter in the warmth of a greenhouse or some similar place. First cut them right down in September and then lift them in October.

Cooking

As a cook you really should never be without tarragon. It has its own very special flavour—subtle yet decisive. Whenever possible it should be included in a bouquet garni.

Tarragon, chervil and chives combined in a salad, omelette or sauce provide an unforgettable and unsurpassable flavour. There are some who have said that the blend of these three herbs is culinary perfection.

Use it in all the creamy sauces, Hollandaise, Bearnaise, Tartare and any fish sauces. I like to use it in stiff bechamels used for filling pancakes, vol-au-vents and other types of pastry cases. It should be made first into an almost dry purée and then blended into the sauce. In this way it can also be used with all creamed vegetables. Blend it into herb butters. Add it to melted butter and use it especially when this is to be served with lobster, prawns and any other shell fish or grilled fish.

I like it with boiled chicken. It flavours both the flesh and the stock. Indeed, it is good with any chicken dish and it improves simple egg and mushroom dishes.

Like basil, tarragon goes well with tomatoes cooked in any way.

Tarragon vinegar used in French dressing brings a subtle flavour to a salad. (See Herb Vinegars.)

Sauce Bearnaise

4tbsp white wine	1tbsp fresh chervil
6tbsp tarragon vinegar	pepper, salt
1tbsp shallots, finely chopped	3 egg yolks
2tbsp finely chopped fresh tarragon	$\frac{1}{2}$lb butter

Put the wine, vinegar, shallot, tarragon, chervil and seasoning into a pan. Bring to the boil and then simmer until the liquid is reduced by two-thirds. Take from the heat. When lukewarm, add the egg yolks one by one, stirring them well. Using either a double saucepan or a very low heat (I recommend the former) and using an egg whisk, beat the mixture constantly, adding the butter little by little. Don't try to hurry this process. When all the butter is used you should have something that looks like a light, warm mayonnaise. Have ready a conical sieve and another pan, a serving saucepan or sauceboat, and quickly strain the sauce through. Add a dash of cayenne pepper and some fresh tarragon and chervil to colour it nicely.

This sauce is served lukewarm. If you try to keep it hot it will curdle.

THYME

Growing
The most useful thymes are the common thyme, *Thymus vulgaris* and the lemon scented thyme, *T. X citriodora*. Both like light, rather dry soils and a warm, sunny place. Both tend to become straggly and un-

tidy, even with fairly frequent gathering, and so are best renewed every three or four years.

Thyme is easily raised from seed which should be sown indoors or in a warm border, in spring. Old plants may also be divided in spring. This is a good and easy way of propagating them.

I think that lemon thyme is best layered. Take a plant and spread its branches out so that they lie on the ground, radiating from the crown. Cover the lower, bare part of the stems with good soil or potting compost so that just the leafy tips are exposed. As time passes the covered stem portions will develop roots. Portions of the plant can then be detached and planted elsewhere.

Quite often you will find portions of thymes of all kinds which have layered naturally. It is quite possible to detach and transplant these.

There are many species of thymes, not all of which come true from seed. Two examples are the English broad-leaved and the French thymes.

Cooking

Common thyme is one of the bouquet garni herbs and should always be included. Fresh thyme can be used more liberally than dried. The latter tends to become dominating.

This is one of our important all-rounder herbs. I can think of few, if any, savoury dishes in which it should not be used. It is particularly good with aubergines, all of the marrow family and especially courgettes, onions and salsify. I like to use it occasionally to give a zest to salads, especially in winter with corn salad.

Lemon thyme is a little more versatile than the common. So much so that it can even be used in certain sweets. Try it in any cream, sorbet or custard in which a lemon flavour is demanded or is acceptable. Try it also in rhubarb pies or with stewed rhubarb.

Sugar can be flavoured with lemon thyme in the same way as for rosemary, see section on rosemary.

TOMATOES

Growing
You can grow tomatoes in unheated greenhouses or out of doors. For greenhouse culture sow seed indoors in warmth from March onwards.

Prick out into individual pots and move on to larger pots when necessary. Plant in cold greenhouse, either in beds or pots or following ring culture methods in late April or early May.

Ring culture is a method using bottomless pots or other containers stood on a 5–6in deep layer of well-weathered ashes. The pots are then filled with John Innes Potting Compost No 2 or No 3 and the plants grown in this, one to a container. Once a fortnight water in some good balanced tomato fertiliser, following carefully the directions given.

Try to have the plants so well grown that the first fruit is already set when they are put in their final positions.

For outdoor culture sow seed indoors in March or April, repot as above and harden off gradually. Plant outdoors during the first week in June in as warm and sheltered a place as possible, preferably against a warm wall, fence or shed.

Plant 1½–2ft apart. Tomatoes may be grown quite well in pots on a patio or a balcony instead of being planted in the open ground. Sugarplum is a new variety good for this purpose. Be sure that pot and ring culture plants do not become dry at the roots. All tomatoes need frequent watering and feeding. Follow the directions given with any fertiliser you buy. There are good specific kinds on the market. Stake well for full support. Remember that the plants have to carry a heavy load at their peak period.

When you can count four flower clusters, nip out the top of the plant to prevent it growing taller and to encourage the fruit to develop. Nip out side shoots, leaving only the flower stems.

The exceptions to this are the bush varieties, such as The Amateur, which stop growing when the fruits ripen. No staking or pinching are required. Incidentally, sow these late, in April, because the plants develop so quickly.

Spray the air around tomatoes every day once they are in flower, for this helps them to pollinate.

If you have to gather green tomatoes at the end of the season, remember that they ripen quicker in the dark.

Cooking
What a versatile food a tomato is! Had you realised that you can cook tomatoes in any way that you cook apples? The only difference is that sometimes you use salt instead of sugar.

As a savoury try a tomato charlotte cooked with a little salt instead of sugar and a sprinkling of basil instead of cinnamon. Try tomatoes as a baked sweet with sugar, each fruit on a little piece of bread which has first been fried crisp in margarine or butter.

Yellow tomatoes, which grow large and sweet in a greenhouse, can be eaten in much the same way as a grapefruit. Cut a slice from the stalk end, sprinkle with either sugar or a little lemon juice according to your taste and eat with a spoon. For a sweet, large ripe fruits can be thinly sliced, sprinkled with sugar and served with yogurt or cream.

Tiny tomatoes can be dipped in fondant the same way as the edible physalis, a member of the same family, but not the one used for flower arrangements. Another kind, little 'currant' tomatoes that grow in long bunches, can be crystallised in the same way as redcurrants. Wash, dry and dip each bunch in egg white and dust with fine sugar. Let them dry and set them on a plate over fresh green mint leaves for summer tea.

Tomato Sauce or Coulis

1tbsp olive oil
1 small onion
1 clove garlic

1 shallot
1lb tomatoes, skinned
salt and pepper

Melt the onions etc in a covered pan in the olive oil. They should soften but not become brown. Add the skinned tomatoes. Simmer for 20min. Test seasoning before serving.

Tomato and Apple Conserve

1lb ripe tomatoes
1lb apples
1 lemon

1½lb sugar
4oz chopped mixed candied peel
4oz chopped ginger

Skin and slice the tomatoes. Peel, core and slice the apples and mince the lemon. Combine all three and cook for 15min. Add the sugar, simmer slowly until the mixture thickens and then add the peel and the ginger. Leave the pan over a very low heat for a further 10min. Put into hot jars and seal. This makes an unusual conserve.

Tomato Ketchup to Bottle

8lb tomatoes
6 medium onions
2 cloves garlic
1 capsicum
2 bay leaves
1tbsp celery seed
1tbsp mustard seed

1tsp peppercorns
1 stick cinnamon
½lb brown sugar
½lb granulated sugar
1pt vinegar
1tbsp lemon juice

Cut up the unskinned tomatoes, onions and garlic (the latter skinned, of course). Put the onions and garlic in a pan, cover with water and boil gently until they are soft and then add the tomatoes, with more water to cover them. Cook until tender. Strain through a sieve. You will find this easier if you first blend all in an electric mixer. Tie the spices in a piece of muslin and add these to the juice, which should now be boiled until it is reduced by half. Warm the sugar and vinegar together and add it with the lemon juice to the tomato liquid. Simmer for about 20min, by which time the sauce should be really thick and about 5qt in volume. Pour into hot jars or bottles and seal.

To Conserve Tomatoes for the Winter

Wash and peel the tomatoes. Put them in a deep saucepan with salt, pepper and a little sugar, say 1tbsp sugar to 1lb tomatoes. Cover and heat them slowly, stirring the fruit from time to time, until all are reduced to a pulp. There should be no hard centre portions remaining.

Put the pulp in a blender or pass it through a sieve. Stir the purée so that it is of an even texture. Pour into storage canisters or plastic bags.

You can keep this also in a refrigerator for some days by pouring some into a jar and covering the top with at least ½in olive oil.

Green Tomato Jam

4lb green tomatoes
4lb sugar
4 cups (2pt) water
2tsp ground ginger

2oz angelica, fresh
1 lemon
1tsp citric acid

Wash the tomatoes and cut into small pieces. Put into a bowl. Sprinkle the sugar over the fruit. Add the water and the ginger. Cover and stand the bowl in a cool place for 48hr. Slice the angelica thinly and mix it with the tomatoes, lemon and citric acid. Put all into a preserving pan, stir and boil for 20–30min until the jam sets. This yields about 5lb of jam.

Green Tomato Pie

Use small fruits and cut a cross at the stem ends. Put them into a pie dish with the juice and the grated rind of half a lemon. Add sugar. Cover with short-crust pastry and bake as for a plum pie. Serve with custard or cream.

If you have a freezer
Remembering all the dishes that call for tomato sauce and purée, freeze plenty of this. I also bake tomatoes whole until they are tender, pack them into containers leaving a little head space and use them later fried, baked or in other ways.

TURNIPS

Growing
Sow these in March and onwards in shallow drills ¾in deep for early crops. For winter, using a different, hardier variety, sow at the end of July and the second week in August. Thin out early to 6in apart.

If you want the plants for their tops rather than their roots, sow in late August or early September. Leave these unthinned.

Cooking
Turnips are sometimes difficult to peel, especially if they are old. Usually, after making an incision, it is possible to pare or even to pull away the outer skin quite cleanly from the tender flesh below. The same applies to swedes.

Cook small turnips whole after peeling them. Divide large ones into quarters. Add them to boiling salted water and simmer until tender. Young roots should take 15–20min, older roots from 45min. Drain well and mash. Add butter, pepper or nutmeg and even all spice.

Stuffed Turnips (serves 4)

8 medium, uniform turnips	1 cup chopped cooked bacon
1 onion	1tbsp breadcrumbs
1 shallot	$\frac{1}{2}$ cup ($\frac{1}{4}$pt) milk
1 clove garlic	salt
1tbsp butter	

Finely chop the onion, shallot and garlic. Peel the turnips and boil in salted water. When tender, drain, cut off a slice from the top of each and scoop out the centres. Chop the pulp, meanwhile, sauté the onion mix in the butter until it is golden. Combine it, the turnip pulp and the bacon together. Add the breadcrumbs to thicken. Fill the turnips and place them in a buttered dish. Put a good pinch of salt in the milk and pour this around the turnips. Bake in a moderate oven until the surfaces are slightly browned.

INDEX